Anthology of Italian Song

Of the Seventeenth and Eighteenth Centuries

Selected and Edited with Biographical Notices by

ALESSANDRO PARISOTTI

English Translations by

DR. THEODORE BAKER

BONONCINI	MARCELLO
CALDARA	MARTINI
CARISSIMI	PAISIELLO
CESTI	PERGOLESI
GLUCK	PICCINNI
HANDEL	A. SCARLATTI
JOMELLI	D. SCARLATTI
LEGRENZI	TRAETTA
LOTTI	VIVALDI

→ Book I . . . . . . Library Vol. 290

Book II . . . . . . Library Vol. 291

ISBN 0-7935-5108-0

G. SCHIRMER, *Inc.*

7777 W. BLUEMOUND RD. P.O. BOX 13819 MILWAUKEE, WI 53213

PREFACE.

WHILE in all art a loving investigation of ancient forms is an unfailing bourn whence flow the most fitting resources for the purification of taste, this applies most fully to music, which, eluding plastic realism, can readily derive from grand models whatever it may need for the improvement and development of its productions. This assertion appears like, and in fact is, a paraphrase of the well-known saying of our great modern melodramatist, the sense of which may perhaps be more directly and forcibly felt in the original general form. And since the new is now-a-days growing scarcer and scarcer, its place may fortunately be filled by the resurrection of the ancient; the more, because it has appeared for some time as if such a resurrection would interest patrons of art far more than current novelties. For these two reasons, then, the time seemed to be ripe for the present publication; and it cannot fail to be a source of real benefit to our beloved art of song, to point out a means for certain improvement both on the æsthetic and practical side. The songs which follow were gleaned from old manuscripts and ancient editions, where they lay in unmerited oblivion. In undertaking this work of exhumation, such an abundance of material was unearthed that the task of rejection, necessitated by the modest proportions of this volume, became difficult and grievous. [Since the above was penned, the very favorable reception accorded to this first volume has encouraged the preparation and publication of a second.] In transcribing the melodies the utmost care was taken to alter nothing in the originals, and often various manuscripts were consulted to ascertain the most elegant and correct form. Obsolete abbreviations were written out in full, and the melodies so selected that none overstep the range of an ordinary voice, thus making them accessible to all. Further, in adding the accompaniments and harmonizing the *bassi continui*, care was taken to insert nothing out of keeping with the words or character of the compositions, or with the style of the author and his period; during this work constant reference was made to the models left by the greatest masters in this style of chamber-music, placed in centuries past at the lofty elevation which is theirs of right.

Having explained the scope of this publication, a few observations on the correct mode of interpreting the music will be offered. The main characteristics peculiar to the composers of the 17th and 18th centuries are clearness and simplicity of form, depth of feeling, and a suave serenity whose grateful influence permeates their entire style. The music of to-day, on the contrary, is neurotic, full of startling effects and violent contrasts. In the interpretation of these ancient songs, therefore, a prime requisite is the avoidance of any exaggeration of *coloris*, of all strained delivery. The singing must be simple, unaffected, tranquil, *legato*; the *tempi* quiet, without any precipitation whatever; the embellishments executed with studious attention, to insure clearness and accuracy; words and tones welded to form one indissoluble whole, so that the hearer cannot fail to comprehend their meaning. The whole delivery; in short, should show delicacy of intuition and a thorough understanding of the laws of the good Italian style; it should be at once calm, elegant, correct, and expressive, yet without coldness or heaviness. No unusual powers are required for singing these ancient songs, though they demand an exact observance of the notes and directions; a modicum of good taste, and a genuine love of study, will do the rest.

Rome, November, 1885.

BIOGRAPHIES OF AUTHORS REPRESENTED IN THIS COLLECTION.

GIOVANNI MARIA BONONCINI.

1640–1678.

By exploring the libraries not a few of Bononcini's works, distinguished by elegance of form and exquisite taste, may be brought to light. Madrigals, symphonies, cantatas and sonatas form a rich and attractive repertory, well worthy of being recalled to life through the agency of the press. But matters are not yet ripe for taking this step, and we must be satisfied if a small portion of these delightful compositions meets with universal approval ; albeit the style of Bononcini is clear, melodious, and unspeakably expressive. In each measure wells up the art of beautiful song ; at every turn are effects surprising in their freshness and aptness.

The arietta printed here was found in an old manuscript of the 18th century, stowed away amidst other gems of the most illustrious Italian composers, in the great library of the Royal Academy of St. Cecilia at Rome. After this manuscript Gavaert edited, in the collection entitled *Gloires d'Italie*, a pleasing melody, "Pietà mio caro bene," which I should have been glad to add to the present series had space not been lacking. Unerringly correct in form, graceful in style, most truthful in the expression of feeling, Bononcini the Modenese, besides being a most eminent composer, was a famous teacher. This is plainly proved by his work, "Il musico pratico" (The practical musician), "a brief demonstration of the manner of attaining a complete knowledge of all those things which belong to the composition of songs and which concern the art of counterpoint," published in 1673. He wrote theatrical works, instrumental pieces, secular sonatas, madrigals, and some cantatas.

He was born about 1640, and died November 19, 1678.

ANTONIO CALDARA.

1670–1736.

He was master of composition to Charles VI, at whose court in Vienna he bore the title of Capellmeister. Previously, he had occupied a similar position at the ducal court in Mantua. An extremely fruitful writer, he left to posterity a long list of sacred and secular works, in all of which the trained hand of the master in art is apparent. The simple and affecting melody, "Come raggio di sol," has lost nothing of its original delicacy and freshness after the lapse of two centuries. Among the numerous cantatas and serenatas from his pen, the pastoral drama entitled *La costanza in amor vince l'inganno* appears peculiarly worthy of mention. Its plot is simple and perfectly idyllic, but the graces of song are lavished throughout with a prodigal hand. He rarely mentions the instruments for the accompaniment, excepting where he writes an *obbligato* for theorbo, *corno da caccia*, the treble viol, etc. In most cases, there is a bare *basso continuo* set underneath the vocal part, with no indication whatever of the harmonization. From the above-mentioned drama we have selected the two ariettas, "Sebben crudele" and "Selve amiche," and should have taken more had space permitted.

Caldara was a pupil of Legrenzi, and enjoyed a higher reputation than his teacher

He set to music libretti by Apostolo Zeno and Pietro Metastasio, among them being *Temistocle.* He was born at Venice in 1670, and died in the same city in 1763.

GIAN GIACOMO CARISSIMI.

1604(?)–1674.

A MORE fitting commencement for this Collection of Ancient Music could hardly be found than a work by a genius of such rare and original type as Carissimi; who, among the great masters of the 17th century, was famous both as a composer and as a teacher of singing. His *Sacrifice of Jephtha* and *Judgment of Solomon,* master-works of the sacred style, founded the grand Italian school continued and extended with such admirable success by his pupils Alessandro Scarlatti and Marco Antonio Cesti. It is much to be regretted that the majority of this fertile author's compositions lie neglected, as dusty and decaying manuscripts, in public libraries, which, possessed of treasures in the shape of scientific and literary works, regard musical writings as poor appendages of slight worth. Hence the difficulty of researches, which might reveal to lovers of art many a hidden treasure and gem of price.

Carissimi, in his life as an artist, was very retiring, and it is not known whether his ppointment to the directorship of the choir in S. Appollinare at Rome brought him greater honor than that at Assisi. However this may be, to his eminent genius and unwearying study of music is due a great advance in musical art, more especially in the style of oratorio and songs.

From among these latter we have selected for publication the one set to the words, *Vittoria, vittoria.* A poor lover has liberated himself from love's bondage, which appears to have been very grievous, and expresses his delight with the most charming vivacity, and in the most elegant form. This song has a character of such marked individuality, that it would be difficult to confound it with other similar compositions.

Carissimi was born at Marino, near Rome, about the year 1604, and died in Rome in 1674. Some biographers contend that he was born at Venice in 1582.

MARCO ANTONIO CESTI.

1620–1669 (?).

AMONG the followers of Carissimi was the monk Fra Marc'Antonio da Arezzo, who was born in that city about 1620, and died at Venice in 1669, or according to others at Rome in 1688. He was a pupil of Carissimi, and one of the foremost composers of the 17th century. His cowl did not hinder him from writing various dramas and amorous cantatas in the style originated by Carissimi, in which aria and recitative alternate, besides many madrigals and secular ariettas.

Not a few of this composer's manuscripts are left us, scattered everywhere through the libraries, and generally neglected. From among these I have been able to select, in the library of the Royal Academy of St. Cecilia and the Chigiana at Rome, a few little songs for three voices with romantic or mythological subjects, and of no mean value, which I hope to see published sooner or later. Cesti's style is wonderfully suave and melodious, and expressive to a degree that might be called sensuous. These features are strongly prominent in the melody "Intorno all' idol mio" belonging to the opera *Orontea,* which was performed in 1649; it may also be found in the fine collection of Carl Banck, entitled *Arien und Gesänge älterer Tonmeister* (Arias and Songs by Earlier Composers).

Numerous other melodies in this author's secular music, with *basso continuo,* deserve to be brought to light, both by reason of their interesting melodic turn and the elegance of their form ; and I propose having them printed in case this first attempt should meet with critical and popular approval.

Cesti was *maestro di cappella* at Florence under Ferdinando III de'Medici, and later assistant Capellmeister to Leopold I at Vienna. His most successful work was the opera *La Dori;* the titles of ten or twelve others are still extant.

CHRISTOPH WILIBALD GLUCK.

1714–1787.

It is with good reason that Gluck is called the reformer of the musical drama; for during the better part of his long career as an artist he devoted all the exceptional powers of his genius to the emancipation of the opera from the shackles of conventional form. In his efforts he met with a redoubtable rival in Piccinni, of whom we shall speak later; so hot was their struggle for supremacy at the French court, that two opposing parties were formed, the Gluckists and the Piccinnists—a striking proof of the interest then taken in art by the public. Piccinni was finally defeated by the immense success attending the performance of Gluck's opera *Iphigenia in Tauris.* The principle at issue in this artistic war was, whether natural dramatic expression in music, as advocated by Lully and Rameau and practically carried out by Gluck, should give way to the mere outward charm of lyrical melody as demanded by the Italian school of singers. Gluck's later operas are masterpieces of true dramatic effect, and the grander the situations, the more boldly does his genius assert itself. At the beginning, however, he was satisfied to follow in the footsteps of the early Italian composers; not until the fiasco of his operas in London (1746) did he seriously address himself to that reformation of his own style which was destined to work a revolution in dramatic music. As a French writer of the time happily put it, "the Italian opera was only a concert for which the drama furnished the pretext." In Gluck's operas, on the other hand, his devotion to truth in dramatic art breathes from every page.

Gluck was born at Weidenwang in the Upper Palatinate on July 25, 1714, studied in Komotow, Prague, Vienna and Milan, in which last-named place his first operas, with Italian words and in the Italian style, were brought out; their success earned him an invitation to London, where the fiasco above alluded to led to the change in his views, which was confirmed by a visit to Paris, where he heard Rameau's operas. The operas, *Alceste* and *Paride ed Elena,* were performed at Vienna in 1767 and 1769 respectively; from the latter is taken the aria "O del mio dolce ardor," in which suave melody, elegance of form, and exquisite dramatic feeling unite to form a rea gem of art. Despite the incontestable beauties of these works, they met with little favor in Vienna; their author consequently removed to Paris, where fame and fortune were the meed of his unwearied efforts He died at Vienna November 15, 1787.

GEORGE FREDERICK HANDEL.

1685–1759.

Handel (properly Georg Friedrich Händel) was born at Halle in Germany on the 23d of February, 1685, not quite a month before Joh. Seb. Bach. His precocious genius attracted the attention of the Duke of Saxe-Weissenfels, who prevailed on his father to provide for his regular instruction in music. At the age of ten he had written a series of sonatas, and in the following year his father journeyed with the youthful composer to Berlin, where his talent for improvisation and playing from a figured bass aroused the admiration of the Italians Bononcini and Ariosti. In 1702 he was appointed organist of the cathedral at Halle, a position which he retained only a year, then going to Hamburg, where his first four operas (in German) were written, *Almira* being especially successful. In 1706 he journeyed to Italy, the home of the opera, and spent over three years in Florence, Rome, and Venice, studying diligently and composing several operas and oratorios in Italian. Thoroughly at home in the Italian vocal style, and already noted as a composer, he came to London in 1710, where he was received with marked distinction; nearly thirty Italian operas written during the ensuing twenty-five years spread his fame far and wide. The opera *Ottone*, from which the arietta "Affanni del pensier" is taken, appeared in 1725; *Alcina*, containing "Ah mio cor, schernito sei," in 1736. Various oratorios, among them *Esther* and *Acis e Galathea*, had also been brought out in the meantime, and met with much favor; besides, Handel had his hands full as a conductor and opera-manager; yet he found time to compose a great number of valuable instrumental works, and made several trips to the continent in search of singers and orchestra-players. His first unquestioned success in oratorio was with the *Messiah*, written in 1741 in twenty-four days; thenceforward he occupied himself almost exclusively with this style of composition, and produced the masterworks which render his fame imperishable. He died at London in 1759, honored and revered in the country of his adoption as no musician before him.

NICCOLA JOMMELLI.

1714–1774.

A PROLIFIC composer in a style peculiarly his own, Niccola Jommelli, one of the foremost opera-writers of the Neapolitan school, was born at Aversa, near Caserta, the 10th of September, 1714, and died at Naples August 25th, 1774. In the last-named city he studied under Durante, Leo, and Mancini, and at Bologna under P. Martini. His name is still a household word in Italy; indeed, on reading any of his compositions, one cannot fail to recognize the stamp of a great genius and of true originality There is something out of the common in Jommelli's music, captivating the hearer by its breadth of conception and the careful working-out of details. At times excessively minutiose, he introduces the flourishes so admired at that period with a lavish hand, as in the celebrated motet *Victimæ paschali*, which, if not the greatest, is certainly one of the most perfect of his works. At all events, he always avoided crudities, and, by combining the charm of novelty with grace of form, has created real works of art. An experience of fourteen years (1754–1768) as Royal Music-Director at Stuttgart, wrought a marked change in his style, which won the applause of the Germans, but which was so little to the taste of the Italians that on his return to Naples his three last —and perhaps best—operas were totally unsuccessful. Jommelli took this cold reception so much to heart, that his death soon followed; his last work was the celebrated *Miserere* for two soprani and orchestra.

He wrote not only operas, but also oratorios, melodramas, masses, motets, requiems, psalms for double chorus, etc. His earlier successes were doubtless due in part to the coöperation of Metastasio, the renowned writer of opera-libretti, concerning whom the following interesting remarks are found in some of Jommelli's letters: "He is a round, fat man of pacific disposition and engaging mien, and with very quiet and elegant manners."—"He is the cleverest artist in adapting music to words of all that I have ever known. If you should ever happen to make his acquaintance, you will be sure to like him; he is certainly the most amiable glutton that ever lived."

GIOVANNI LEGRENZI.

1625–1690.

Of this composer who was born at Clusone near Bergamo in 1625, and died at Venice, where he was *maestro di cappella* in San Marco, in 1690, seventeen theatrical works, and numerous masses, motets and psalms, concertos, sonatas, and cantatas are extant. He was one of the first to write trios for two violins and 'cello, and enjoyed the reputation of being one of the best composers of the 17th century. He was the director of the ducal musicians at Ferrara, and of the Conservatorio de'Mendicanti at Venice; he considerably enlarged the orchestra of St. Mark's, raising the number of players to thirty-four (eight violins, eleven small viols, two tenor viols, three viole da gamba and contrabass viols, four theorbos, two cornetti, one bassoon, and three trombones). The selected arietta "Che fiero costume," taken from the opera *Etocle,* and effeminate like nearly all the poetry of the period, lacks neither freshness nor boldness, qualities on which changes of fashion have no hold. Its effect is charming, and the style chaste throughout. It therefore appears to me not to be out of place in this collection. Pupils of Legrenzi were Antonio Caldera and Antonio Lotti. It is claimed by some that he wore priestly vestments.

ANTONIO LOTTI.

1667–1740.

A pupil of Giovanni Legrenzi, and his successor as music-director at San Marco in Venice, Lotti was an eminent composer of sacred music and operas; his first opera, *Giustino,* was brought out at Venice when he was but sixteen years of age. An expert in the art of handling the voice, which was his favorite department of music, he founded a celebrated school of singing at Venice. Among his pupils were Benedetto Marcello, Galuppi (Buranello), and other fine musicians. He outstripped his teacher not only in fertility of invention, but in beauty or form and the expression of emotion, and ranks among the foremost original artists of the time. In the arietta "Pur dicesti, o bocca bella," simplicity, clearness, and infinite grace are so happily combined, as still to challenge our admiration.

His knowledge of the art of singing is apparent throughout this composition, and particularly in the effects of the portamento and syncopation, the elegant style, and a wise economy in the management of coloratura and embellishments. Some biographers assert that Lotti was born at Hanover in 1667, of Venetian parents, his father being music-director at the Electoral Court; others say that he was born at Venice in 1665; he died at Venice January 5, 1740.

BENEDETTO MARCELLO.

1686–1739.

The work "Estro poetico-armonica," better known now-a-days under the title of Psalms of Marcello, rendered its author famous among his contemporaries, and secured the admiration of posterity. He was a *littérateur* and poet of considerable merit, and wrote a *Treatise on musical theory according to modern practice,* the *Teatro alla moda,* a poem, *Arato in Sparta,* and other literary works. In his capacity as a musician he composed oratorios, cantatas, serenatas, masses, motets, etc., written in a severe style, but filled with the inspiration of true genius. The arietta "Quella fiamma che m'accende" is characterized by its smooth and tasteful style; its harmony has a graceful and original turn, and the general effect is excellent. In Banck's Collection it is quoted several times.

Benedetto Marcello was a pupil of Lotti, a sketch of whom is given above, and o Francesco Gasparini of Lucca. He was born at Venice of noble family, on August the 1st, 1686; studied law, becoming a barrister, and for fourteen years was one of the council of Forty; removed to Pola, where he held the post of *provveditore* for eight years, contracting in that fatal climate the germs of a malady which ended his life in 1739. He secretly married a girl of obscure origin, one of his pupils, having fallen desperately in love with her. In the church of San Giuseppe dei Franciscani at Brescia the following inscription may be found on his tomb:

BENEDICTO MARCELLO
SCIENTISSIMO PHILOLOGO
POETÆ
MUSICES PRINCIPI.

GIOVANNI MARTINI.

1741–1816.

THE lovely melody "Piacer d'amor" has frequently been attributed to the celebrated Padre Martini (Giambattista Martini), the author of the *Storia della musica;* but the most careful editors, among them Banck in his Collection, have cast doubts upon his authorship, and it would now appear settled that its writer was Jean Paul Egide Schwarzendorf, who was born at Freistadt in the Palatinate, and, on removing to Nancy in 1760, Italianized his name, in accordance with a fashion not yet obsolete. His career was replete with curious adventures. At the age of ten he became organist of the Jesuit seminary at Neuburg, where he was inscribed as a student; seven years later we find him organist in the Franciscan church at Freiburg, where he decided to devote himself wholly to music. Not knowing whither to betake himself, he resorted to the expedient of ascending a high tower, from the top of which he let fall a feather; as the feather drifted towards France, he started for Nancy, without a penny in his pocket. On the way he found shelter in various cloisters, in which his skill as an organist won him favorable attention. In Nancy he obtained a situation in the workshops of the organ-builder Dupont, who, recognizing his genius, generously aided him. He changed his name, as mentioned above, and became a music-teacher (1760); four years later he proceeded to Paris, where his success in a competitive composition of a march earned him high protection, through which he was appointed officer *à la suite* of a cavalry regiment, the leisure thus obtained being at first employed in writing military music. In 1771, however, he composed an opera entitled *L'amoureux de quinze ans*, a work marking the beginning of a brilliant career. He became noted and popular under the name of Martini the German; the Prince of Condé made him his *maître de chapelle*, a post exchanged later for a similar one under the Count of Artois; after the vicissitudes of the Revolution, he finally secured the position of Intendant of the Conservatory. He died at Paris in 1816.

A talented composer and distinguished harmonist, he wrote twelve operas, various masses, requiems, psalms and other sacred compositions, six quartets for flute with string trio, twelve trios for two violins with 'cello, etc., etc., besides numerous instruction-books. Fétis says of him: "His melodies were expressive and dramatic; his romances, preceding those of Garat and Boieldieu, may be regarded as models of their kind, and that which he wrote on the words *Plaisir d'amour* will always be quoted as a *chef d'œuvre* of grace and gentle melancholy."

GIOVANNI PAISIELLO.

1741–1816.

PAISIELLO was one of the brightest stars of the 18th century; eminent as a composer of opera, and especially so as a writer of *opera buffa*, he also tried his hand at nearly every other style of musical composition, and in all was both elegant and powerful, simple, yet original. From his native town of Taranto, where he was born May

9, 1741, he went to Naples, studying there for five years as a pupil of Durante, when he received an appointment as assistant teacher at the Conservatorio Sant' Onofrio; the immense success of a comic intermezzo written by him, and performed in the theatre of the Conservatory, brought in its train a host of orders from the theatres. Nearly one hundred operas were the fruit of his artistic career, which from beginning to end was a series of almost uninterrupted triumphs. His musical setting of "The Barber of Seville" enjoyed such extraordinary popularity, that when Rossini ventured to compose the same subject there were not a few who prophesied his failure. Among his best operas may be mentioned *La bella Molinara, Gli Zingari in fiera,* and *Nina pazza per amore,* from the first of which the arietta "Nel cor più non mi sento," from the second the canzone "Chi vuol la zingarella," and from the third the aria "Il mio ben," are taken. The genuine musical value of these little gems will sufficiently recommend them to all lovers of *il bel canto.*

Like so many of the leading Italian musicians of the period, Paisiello spent a considerable portion of his life in foreign lands, chiefly in Paris and St. Petersburg; at the time of his decease he held the position of Director of the Conservatory at Naples.

GIOVANNI BATTISTA PERGOLESI.

1710–1736.

WHO could read unmoved the touching story of the death of this swan of Jesi? His career, unlike that of so many Italian composers of the time, whose works were during their lives lauded to the skies, only to meet with oblivion after their death, was a series of bitter disappointments; not until he had passed away did his compositions find the recognition they deserved. He was born at Jesi, January 4, 1710, and at a very early age was admitted to the Conservatorio dei Poveri at Naples; his original improvisations on the violin attracted attention, and secured him careful instruction from such teachers as Durante and Francesco Feo; far from adopting their style, however, he formed one of his own, in which melody and expression were not sacrificed to contrapuntal science. His last school-work, a sacred drama entitled "The Conversion of San Guglielmo," performed with comical intermezzi at the cloister of San Agnello, and also his two first operas of the same year, appear to have had little success; but a series of trios written for a princely and intelligent patron paved the way to a commission from the king to write a solemn mass dedicated to the patron saint of Naples, on occasion of a violent earthquake; the favorable reception of this mass encouraged further attempts in the same line, which made his name known in that city, at least. His most celebrated operetta, or rather intermezzo, *La serva padrona,* was written in 1731, but despite the delightful freshness of the music and the novelty (at that time) of the plot, it made scarcely any impression; several other operas brought out in succession met with a similar fate. The indifference shown to his compositions, a weak constitution, and (it is said) an unhappy love-affair, combined to undermine his health to such an extent that he was forced to seek relief in the sea-baths of Pozzuoli; but his strength was too far exhausted, and death terminated his woes on April the 17th, 1736. The last work from his pen was the justly renowned *Stabat mater,* which he finished on his death-bed, and for which he received the munificent remuneration of ten ducats (42½ florins).

The arietta "Stizzoso, mio stizzoso," from *La serva padrona,* bears the stamp of original genius in its graceful, sparkling melody and admirable comic effect, and is a fine specimen of the naturalness and originality of Pergolesi's style.

NICCOLÒ PICCINNI.

1728–1800.

THIS celebrated rival of Gluck, already mentioned in the sketch of the latter, was born at Bari in 1728; a stroke of paralysis caused his death at Passy, in 1800. The aria selected for publication is taken from the opera *Le faux Lord*, and is well calculated to show the genius of its author. The freshness of the melodic movement and the discreet use of harmonic resources render it difficult to believe that the music was actually written more than a century ago. Admitting that Gluck, his successful rival, was a master in orchestral color and strong dramatic passion, Piccinni was assuredly no less great in harmonic resources and in the true expression of the tenderest emotion. He was one of the most prolific opera-composers who have ever lived; he wrote over one hundred and fifty dramatic works, which were extremely popular both in France and Italy. A pupil of Leo and Durante, he followed faithfully in their footsteps, merely broadening, as the progress of art required, the horizon of the melodic and instrumental forms. His kindly and genial nature neither allowed him to take part in the intrigues at the French court, where his adherents endeavored to compass Gluck's downfall, nor to feel any bitterness at the success of his competitor for the public favor. And later in life, when death had removed his redoubtable rival Sacchini from the court of Vienna, Piccinni held, at the funeral, a discourse full of the most generous praise for the eminent composer. He has been called the father of *opera buffa*, a titled merited, in particular, by reason of the exquisite construction of all his works in that style. Though high in favor at the court of Marie Antoinette, the difficulties which he naturally encountered in setting a foreign language to music would seem to account, at least in part, for his ultimate ill-success. His most unfortunate venture was, undoubtedly, the attempt to compose *Iphigenia in Tauris,* in opposition to Gluck's masterpiece; which latter finally drove Piccinni from the field.

ALESSANDRO SCARLATTI.

1659–1725.

POTENT in artistic conception, of most fertile and versatile genius, Alessandro Scarlatti, the illustrious founder of the Neapolitan school, was not only a great composer, but equally great as a singer and as a player on the harp and harpsichord. Himself the pupil of Carissimi, his own most celebrated pupils were Leo, Pergolesi, and Durante, to whom he bequeathed an innumerable host of masses (200), operas (106), oratorios, cantatas, madrigals, motets, toccatas, serenades, etc. He was *maestro di cappella* at the Neapolitan court, and later at the cathedral of Santa Maria Maggiore in Rome; afterwards returning to Naples, where he also acted as Director of a conservatory. In his compositions a flowing style is united with elegance, yet simplicity, of form. He was the first to introduce the *da capo* into the grand aria (in his opera *Teodora*, brought out at Rome in 1693). Most of his compositions are written over a *basso continuo* with or without figures, and his style is always correct, simple, and expressive. Though the modulations are somewhat bold for his period, clearness never suffers thereby. He was born at Trapani, Sicily, in 1659, and died at Naples October 24, 1725.

"O cessate di piagarmi" and "Se tu della mia morte" well exhibit his power of appealing to the feelings; and the arietta "Spesso vibra per suo giuoco" shows with what elegance he could write in the semi-serious vein.

DOMENICO SCARLATTI.

1685–1757.

THE son of Alessandro Scarlatti, some of whose graceful songs we have also printed, he was likewise his pupil, also studying under Gasparini. His fame was established while he was still a young man, and, as commonly the case in Italy at that period, by the performance of his operas; but for coming generations it is founded chiefly upon his unquestioned eminence as a player on and writer for the harpsichord. He also earned laurels as an organ-player, and at the time of Handel's visit to Rome (1709), was pitted against the latter by Cardinal Ottoboni. Among the multitude of his excellent compositions we note the curious *Fuga del gatto* (Cat-fugue), suggested by a cat's running across the keys of his harpsichord while he sat at work. Besides instrumental works he wrote not a few vocal compositions, among which may be mentioned several operas, a mass for four vocal parts and orchestra, a *Salve regina* with string-quartet, and some secular arias. Of these last the "Consolate e spera" strikes me as being remarkably attractive;—the movement is highly dramatical, and consequently the melody is certain to prove effective. It is also to be found in the collection of *Arien und Gesänge* noticed before.

In 1715 Scarlatti was appointed *maestro di cappella* at St. Peter's in Rome, which sufficiently shows the estimation in which he was held; he was also teacher of the harpsichord to the Princess of Asturia in Madrid from 1746 to 1754, then returning to Naples. His son Giuseppe was likewise a musician of note. Domenico was born at Naples in 1683, and died there in 1757 (or, according to other authorities, in Madrid).

TOMMASO TRAETTA.

1727–1779.

From the masterpiece of this composer, the *Antigone*, I have taken the scena and aria "Ombra cara, amorosa," the wondrous pleading of whose melodies and harmonies shows the height to which the great Italian composers of the 18th century carried the art of melodramatic expression. In the aria, as in the grand *scena* preceding it, the music seems wedded to the words; the *scena* has the broad form of an arioso, and is worthy of a place here as a model of its kind.

Traetta, a shining light of the Neapolitan school, was born at Bitonto, near Naples; for ten years (1738-1748) he studied under Durante, and his first opera, *Il Farnace*, which was brought out in 1750, met with remarkable favor, so that its fortunate author was immediately overwhelmed with orders from Italian theatres, in consequence of which he threw off opera after opera with almost careless haste. In 1758 he became music-director and court teacher at Parma, went to Venice in 1765, and three years later to St. Petersburg, where he stayed till 1776; thence he proceeded to London, where he met with a very cool reception, Sacchini being at that time the accepted favorite of court and public; he at length returned to Italy, and died on the 6th of April, 1779, at Venice.

ANTONIO VIVALDI.

16—(?)–1743.

Antonio Vivaldi, surnamed *il prete rosso* (the red priest) from the color of his hair, was born at Venice in the second half of the 17th century, and died there in 1743 as the Director of the *Conservatorio della Pietà*. He took holy orders while young, and became later a celebrated violinist and composer of dramatic and instrumental works. He wrote no less than twenty-eight operas, besides many trios, sonatas, and concertos for the violin and other instruments. The arietta "Un certo non so che" is a beautiful example of graceful expression and style, as well as of pleasing originality. Vivaldi held for some time a position as violinist at the court of the Elector Philip of Hesse-Darmstadt. The following curious anecdote is related of him:

While celebrating the mass one day, a sudden musical inspiration of such beauty seized him that he felt unable to let it go unnoticed; carried away by artistic enthusiasm, he stopped short in the midst of the holy office, retired into the sacristy, and wrote down the fugitive thought. Having done so, he quietly returned to the altar, and finished the interrupted mass. For this dereliction of duty he was summoned before the tribunal of the Holy Inquisition. Fortunately his judges, anticipating the modern theory of delinquency, pronounced him mad; hence his punishment was limited to prohibiting him thenceforward from celebrating the mass.

CONTENTS

Vittoria, mio core!

(Victorious my heart is!)

Cantata.

English Version by
H. MILLARD.

GIAN GIACOMO CARISSIMI.
(1604(?)-1674)

p
cresc.
sciolta_ d'A - mo - re_ La_ vil ser - vi - tù, È sciol - - -
love now has bro - ken its shackles in twain, For love
sf
p
cresc.
f
- - - - ta d'A - mo - re La ser - vi - tù.
now has bro - ken its shackles in twain.
f f f
sf
meno mosso, e dolce assai.
p
Già l'em - pia a' tuoi dan - ni Fra stuo - lo di sguar - di, Con vez - zi bu -
The false one is vanquish'd, her glances a - muse me, De - ception no
p meno mosso, e dolce assai.
cresc.
giar - di Di - spo - se_ gl'in - gan - - - ni; Le fro - de, gli af -
longer with arts can_ con - fuse_ me! No false - hood or
cresc.

fan-ni Non han-no più lo - - co, Del cru - do suo fo - co È
sorrow op - press me with rig - - or, The flame, once so cru - el, has
Tempo I.
spen-to_ l'ar - do - - re! Vit - to - ria! Vit - to - ria! Vit-
spent all_ its_ vig - - or! Vic - to - rious! Vic - to - rious! Vic -
to-ria! Vit - to - ria, mio co - - re! Non la - grimar più, Non
torious! Vic - to-rious my heart is! And tears are in vain, And
la - gri-mar più, È sciol-ta d'A - mo - re La vil ser - vi -
tears are in vain, For love now has bro-ken its shack-les in

p
cresc.
f
tù, È sciol - - - - - - ta d'A-
twain, For love now has
p
cresc.
f f
mo-re La ser - vi - tu! Da lu-ci ri-den-ti Non e - sce più
broken its shackles in twain! Her smile once en - trancing no darts is re -
meno mosso, e dolce assai.
f f f
p meno mosso, e dolce assai.
strale, Che pia-ga mor-ta-le Nel pet-to m'av-ven - ti: Nel
vealing, The wounds in my bo-som with time are all heal - - ing; All
cresc.
duol, ne' tor-menti lo più non mi sfac - cio E rot-to o-gni
sorrow and torment no lon-ger I'm fear - ing, Now bro-ken each
cresc.

Tempo I.
lac-cio, Spa - ri - to il ti - mo - re! Vit - to-ria! Vit - to-ria! Vit-
tie is, all fears dis - ap - pear - ing! Vic - to-rious, Vic - to-rious, Vic-
to-ria! Vit - to-ria, mio co - re! Non la - grimar più, Non la - grimar
torious, Vic - to-rious my heart is! And tears are in vain, And tears are in
più, È sciol - ta d'A - mo - re La vil ser - vi - tù, È sciol - -
vain, For love now has bro-ken its shackles in twain, For love
cresc.
largamente stent.
- - - - ta d'A - mo-re La ser - vi - tù!
now has broken its shackles in twain!
cresc.
col canto

Intorno all'idol mio.
(Caressing mine idol's pillow.)
Aria.

English Version by
Dr TH. BAKER.

MARCO ANTONIO CESTI.
(1620 - 1669(?))

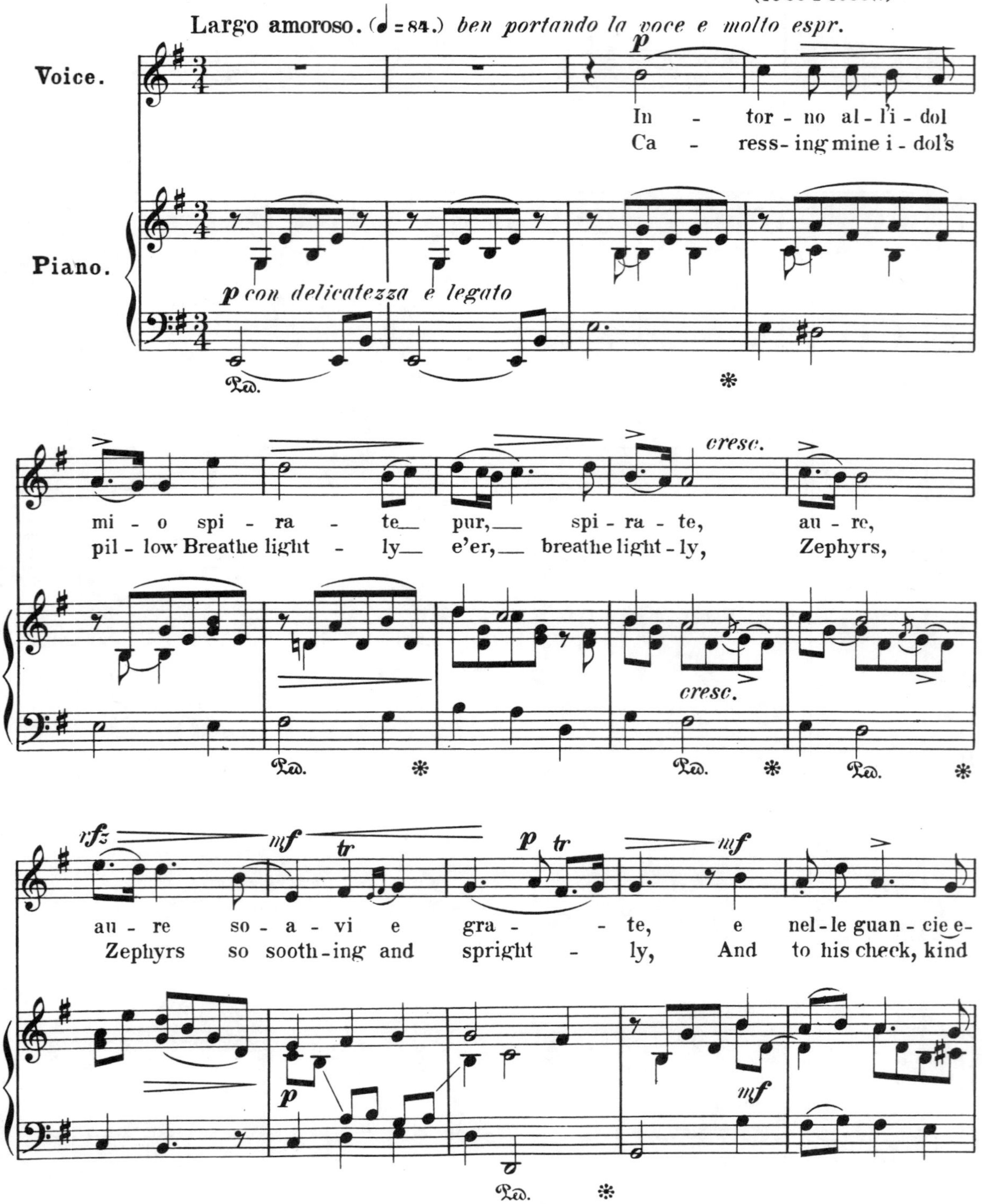

Largo amoroso. (♩= 84.) *ben portando la voce e molto espr.*

Voice.

Piano.

p con delicatezza e legato

In - tor - no al - l'i - dol mi - o spi - ra - te pur, spi - ra - te, au - re, au - re so - a - vi e gra - te, e nel - le guan - cie e-

Ca - ress - ing mine i - dol's pil - low Breathe light - ly e'er, breathe light - ly, Zephyrs, Zephyrs so sooth - ing and spright - ly, And to his cheek, kind

cresc.
rfz
più cresc.
let - te ba - cia - te - lo per me, cor - te - si, cor -
breez - es, In greet - ing bear from me, The__ sweet - est, the
Ped. *
rfz
p
poco rit.
te - si au - ret - - - te! e nel - le guan - cie e -
sweet - est of kiss - - - es! And to his cheek, kind
rfz
p smorz.
poco rit.
smorz.
cresc.
let - te ba - cia - te - lo per me, ba - cia - te - lo per me, cor -
breezes, In greet - ing bear from me, in greet - ing bear from me the
rfz
p
rit.
tr
te - si, cor - te - si au - ret - - te!
sweet - est, the__ sweet - est of__ kiss - - es!
col canto pp

mf
cresc.
Al mio ben, che ri - po - sa su l'a - - li
To my love, who his spir - it to rest - ful
p
dim.
cresc.
rfz
del - la qui - e - te, gra - ti, gra - ti
night doth sur - ren - der, Waft ye, waft ye
poco rit.
tr
p
so - gni as - si - ste - - te E il mio racchiu - so ar -
fair dreams and ten - - der, And all my pas - sion re -
poco rit.
più cresc.
do - re sve - la - te - gli per me, o lar - ve, o
press - ed Re - veal to him for me, O vis - ion, O
cresc.

rfz portando
pp
tr
mf
lar - ve d'a - mo - - re, e il
vis - ion so ___ bless - - - ed! And
rfz
p
mf
mio rac-chiu - so ar - do - re sve - la - te-gli per me, sve -
all my pas - sion re-press-ed Re - veal to him for me, re -
decresc.
cresc.
rfz
la - te-gli per me, o ___ lar - ve, o lar - ve d'a -
veal to him for me, O ___ vis - ion, O vis - ion so
cresc.
rit.
mo - - re! ___
bless - - ed! ___
p col canto
p
dim.
pp

Che fiero costume.

(How void of compassion.)

Arietta.

English Version by
Dr TH. BAKER.

GIOVANNI LEGRENZI.
(1625 _ 1690)

mf un poco meno
rfz
E pur nell' ar-do-re il dio tra-di-to-re un
And yet in my ar-dor I fol-low the hard-er The
f
un poco meno
rfz
espr.
dol.
p
va-go sembiante mi fe'i-do-la-trar, un va-go sembian-te mi
vi-sion e-lu-sive he shadows be-fore, The vi-sion e-lu-sive he
f
p
rit.
Tempo I.
sfz
decresc.
fe'i-do-la-trar. Che fie-ro cos-tu-me d'a-li-ge-ro nu-me, che a
shadows be-fore. How void of compassion Is Cu-pid his fashion, Who
più f
rit.
ten.
sfz
p
cresc.
f
mf
for-za di pe-ne si fac-cia a-do-rar, si faccia a-do-rar! che a
drives me by torment himself to a-dore, him-self to a-dore! Who
cresc.
sfz
f

for - za di pe - ne si fac - cia a - do - rar!
drives me by torment him - self to a - dore!
Che cru - do de - sti - no che un cie - co bam - bi - no con
O Des - ti - ny senseless! A boy so defenceless, Scarce
boc - ca di lat - te si fac - cia stimar, si fac - cia sti - mar, con
wean'd, yet can make us his fa - vor implore, his fa - vor im - plore, Scarce
boc - ca di lat - te si fac - cia sti - mar!
wean'd, yet can make us his fa - vor im - plore!

mf un poco meno
rfz
Ma que - sto ti - ran - no con bar - ba - ro ingan - no, en -
A ty - ran - nous mentor, Our eyes he doth en - ter With
f
un poco meno
rfz
espr.
dol.
p
tran - do per gli occhi, mi fe' so - spi - rar,
en - tran - do per gli occhi mi
bar - bar - ous wiles till we sigh and give o'er,
With bar - bar - ous wiles till we
rit.
Tempo I.
sfz
decresc.
fe' so - spi - rar.
Che cru - do de - sti - no che un
sigh and give o'er.
O Des - ti - ny sense - less! A
rit.
più f
ten.

cie - co bam - bi - no con boc - ca di lat - te si fac - cia sti - mar, si
boy so de - fence-less, Scarce wean'd, yet can make us his fa - vor im - plore, his
fac - cia sti - mar! con boc - ca di lat - te si
fa - vor im - plore! Scarce wean'd, yet can make us his
fac - cia sti - mar!
fa - vor im - plore!
col canto
cresc.

Deh più a me non v'ascondete.
(Ah! why let me ever languish.)
Arietta.

English Version by
Dr. TH. BAKER.

GIOVANNI MARIA BONONCINI.
(1640 - 1703)

rit.
sol, lu - ci va - ghe del mio sol, lu - ci va - ghe del mio
Sun, In thy way-ward beams,my Sun, In thy way - ward beams,my
rit.
sol.
Sun?
p
Con sve - lar - vi, se voi
Clear out - shin - ing, thou canst
p dol.
p
rit.
sie - te, voi po - te - te far que - st'al-ma fuor di duol. voi po -
ban-ish All the anguish Of the night my soul doth shun, All the
rit.
dim.
rit.
te - te far que-st'al-ma fuor di duol, far quest'al-ma fuor di duol.
an - guish of the night my soul doth shun, of the night my soul doth shun.
p dol.

p
Deh, più a me non v'a-scon - de - te, lu - ci va-ghe del mio
Ah why let me ev - er languish In thy waywardbeams,my
p
sol, deh, più a me non v'a-scon - de - te, lu - ci va-ghe del mio
Sun? Ah why let me ev - er languish In thy waywardbeams,my
p
sol, lu - ci va - ghe del mio sol, lu - ci va - ghe del mio
Sun, in thy way - ward beams, my Sun, in thy way-ward beams,my
molto rit.
sol, lu-ci va - ghe del mio sol.
Sun, in thy way - ward beams,my Sun?
col canto
p
ff

O cessate di piagarmi.

(O no longer seek to pain me.)

Arietta.

English Version by
Dr TH. BAKER.

ALESSANDRO SCARLATTI.
(1659 - 1725)

poco a poco
di - spie - ta - te, più del ge - lo e più del mar - mi
so un - grate - ful; Ice nor stone could so dis - dain me,
dim.
p
smorz.
pp
fred - de e sor - de a' miei mar - tir, fred - de e sor - de a'
Nor so cold - ly hear my cry, nor so cold - ly
rit.
mf dolente ed appassionato.
miei mar - tir. O ces - sa - te di pia - gar - mi,
hear my cry. Or no long - er seek to pain me,
mf
con dolore e ritenuto assai
o la - scia - te - mi mo - rir, o la - scia - te - mi mo - rir.
Or give o'er, and let me die, Or give o'er, and let me die.
rit. assai
La seconda volta
molto ritenuto

Se Florindo è fedele.

(Should Florindo be faithful.)

Arietta.

English Version by
Dr. TH. BAKER.

ALESSANDRO SCARLATTI.
(1659 - 1725)

mo - re - rò, s'è fe - de - le Flo - rin - do m'in -
fall in love; Should Flo - rin - do be faith - ful I'll
cresc.
dolce
na - mo - re - rò, io m'in - na - mo - re - rò, s'è fe -
sure-ly fall in love, I'll sure - ly fall in love; If Flo -
de - le Flo - rin - do m'in - na - mo - re - rò,
rin - do be faith - ful I'll sure - ly fall in love,
rall.
m'in - na - mo - re - rò, m'in - na - mo - re - rò,
I shall fall in love, I shall fall in love,
col canto
imitando la voce

f a tempo
p dolce
io m'in - na - mo - re - rò.
I'll sure-ly, sure-ly fall in love.
f a tempo
p
p
Po - trà ben l'ar-co ten - de-re il fa - re -
How art - ful e'er he draw the bow, Well - vers'd in
fp
tra-to ar - cier, ch'io mi sa-prò di-fen - de-re d'un
arch-ers' wiles, My heart I can de-fend, I know, From
fp
fz
f
p
pp
guar - do lu - sin - ghier. Pre - ghi,
a - ny lur-ing smiles. Sigh - ing,
cresc.
p

pian - ti e que - re - le, io non a - scol - te - rò,
weep-ing, and im - plor - ing My breast can nev - er move;
pp
p
con grazia
ma se sa - rà fe - de - le, ma se sa - rà fe - de - le io
But if he should be faithful, but if he should be faith - ful I'll
m'in - na - mo - re - rò, io m'in - na - mo - re -
sure - ly fall in love, I'll sure - ly fall in
p
dolce
rall.
rò, m'in - na - mo - re - rò, m'in - na - mo - re -
love, I shall fall in love, I shall fall in
p
col canto
imitando il canto

a tempo
rò, io m'in - na - mo - re - rò, se Flo -
love, I'll sure - ly, sure - ly fall in love; Should Flo -
a tempo
rin - do è fe - de - le io m'in - na - mo - re - rò,
rin - do be faith - ful I'll sure - ly fall in love;
se Flo - rin - do è fe - de - le
Should Flo - rin - do be faith - ful
cresc.
io m'in - na - mo - re - rò, s'è fe - de - le Flo -
I'll sure - ly fall in love; Should Flo - rin - do be
cresc.

rin - do m'in - na - mo - re - rò, io m'in - na - mo - re -
faith - ful I'll sure - ly fall in love, I'll sure - ly fall in
rò, s'è fe - de - le Flo - rin - do m'in - na - mo - re -
love; Should Flo - rin - do be faith - ful I'll sure - ly fall in
rall.
rò, m'in - na - mo - re - rò, m'in - na - mo - re -
love, I shall fall in love, I shall fall in
col canto
imitando la voce
rit. assai
rò, io m'in - na - mo - re - rò.
love, I'll sure - ly, sure - ly fall in love!
rit. assai

Son tutta duolo.

(Desponding, lonely.)

Aria.

English Version by
Dr. TH. BAKER.

ALESSANDRO SCARLATTI.
(1659 - 1725)

e per me so - lo so - no ti - ran - ni gli a - stri, la
And me, me on - ly Mock in mine an - guish All stars in
sor - te, i nu - mi il ciel, e per me so -
heav - en, The gods, and Fate, and me, me on -
lo so - no ti - ran - ni gli a - stri, la sor - te, i nu -
ly mock in mine an - guish all stars in heav - en, the gods,
mi, i nu - mi il ciel, i nu - mi il ciel.
the gods, and Fate, the gods, and Fate.
cresc.
cresc.

p
Son tut - ta duo -
De - sponding, lone -
ff
p
lo, non ho che af - fan - ni
ly I here must lan - guish,
mf
mf
f
lento
e mi dà mor - te pe - na cru - del, pe - na cru - del,
Sore wounded e - ven For death I wait, for death I wait;
f
f p
mf
f
stent.
rit.
e mi dà mor - te pe - na cru - del, pe - na cru - del.
Sore wounded e - ven For death I wait, for death I wait.
f
stent.
f col canto

Spesso vibra per suo gioco.

(Oft the blindfold boy.)

Canzonetta.

English Version by
Dr. TH. BAKER.

ALESSANDRO SCARLATTI.
(1659 - 1725)

Allegro. (♩. = 126.)

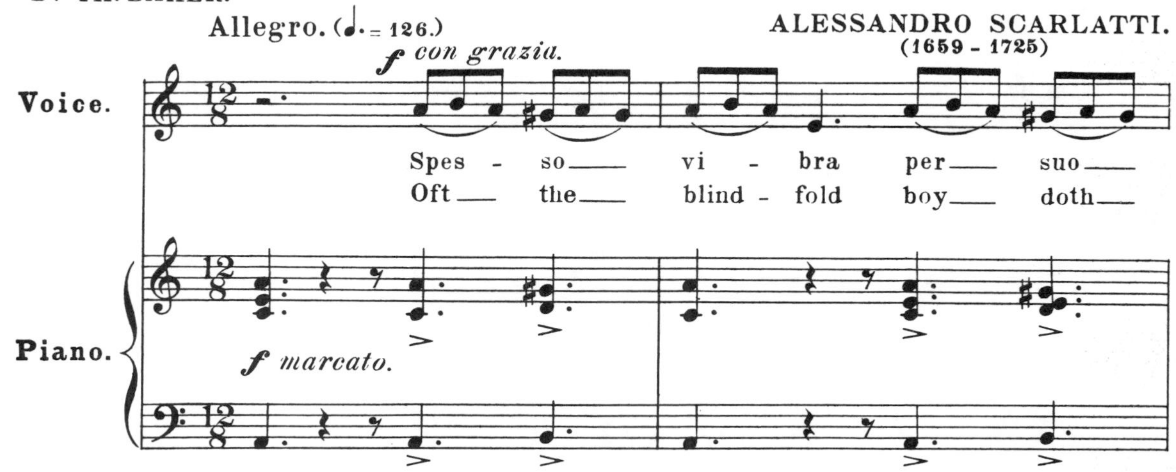

a tempo.
rall.
re, stral di fer - ro in no - bil co - - re.
ic, darts of steel for hearts he - ro - - ic.
a tempo.
p rall.
f a tempo.
cresc.
Poi lan - guen-do in mez - zo al fo - co del di - - ver - so ac - ce - - so stra - le per og - - get - to non e - -
Then con - sum-ed by fire they languish Of his fiercely en-kin - dled ar - rows, Old or young, a - like their
cresc.

gua - le que - - - - sto man - - - - ca, que - - - - sto
sor - rows, None so bold, no, none so
man - - ca e quel vien me - - - - no, que - - - sto
cold, can play the sto - - ic, none so
rit assai.
man - - ca, que - - sto man - ca e quel vien me - - no.
bold, no, none so cold can play the sto - ic.
col canto.
Spes - so vi - bra per - suo
Oft the blind - fold boy doth
f marcato.

più f
gio - co il ben - da - to par - go - let - to stra - li d'o - ro in u - mil pet - to, stral di fer - ro in no - bil se - no, stral di fer - ro in no - bil se - no.
bran - dish, While in play - ful mood he hov - ers, Shafts of gold for low - ly lov - ers, Darts of steel for hearts he - ro - ic, Darts of steel for hearts he - ro - ic.
cresc.
p
f
rall.
p col canto.
a tempo.
p rall. assai.

Se tu della mia morte.

(Would'st thou the boast of ending.)

Aria.

English Version by
Dr. TH. BAKER.

ALESSANDRO SCARLATTI.
(1659 - 1725)

p
la a'tuoi lu - mi.
it to thine own eyes.
p
Se tu del-la mia mor-te a
Would'st thou the boast of end-ing A
p
f
que-sta de-stra for - te la glo-ria non vuoi dar,
life and love of-fend-ing De - ny to this right hand,
mf
p
dal - - - la, dal - la a'tuoi lu - - mi,
Grant it to thine, to thine own eyes,
p
f
p
rit. con grazia.
dal - - - la, dal - la a'tuoi lu - - mi,
Grant it to thine, to thine own eyes;
rit. col canto.
sf

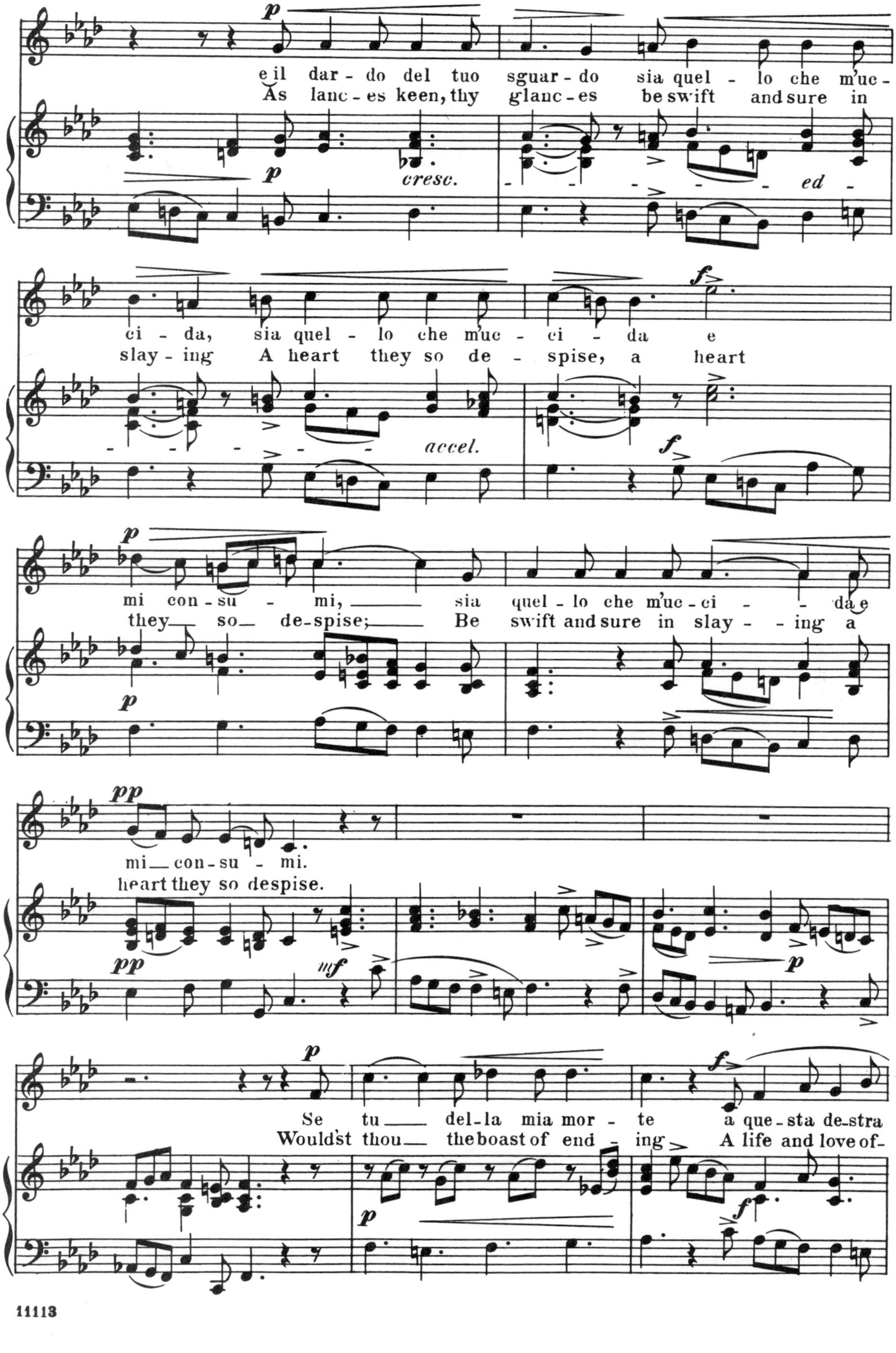

e il dar - do del tuo sguar - do sia quel - lo che m'uc -
As lanc - es keen, thy glanc - es be swift and sure in

ci - da, sia quel - lo che m'uc - ci - da e
slay - ing A heart they so de - spise, a heart

mi con - su - mi, sia quel - lo che m'uc - ci - da e
they so de - spise; Be swift and sure in slay - ing a

mi con - su - mi.
heart they so despise.

Se tu del - la mia mor - te a que - sta de - stra
Would'st thou the boast of end - ing A life and love of -

p
for - te la glo - ria non vuoi dar, dal - la a'tuoi lu -
fend - ing De - ny to this right hand, Grant it to thine own
mi, dal - - - - la a'tuoi lu - - mi.
eyes, grant it to thine own eyes.
p
p
f
Se tu del - la mia mor - te a
Would'st thou the boast of end - ing A
f
cresc.
que - sta de - stra for - te la glo - ria non vuoi dar, dal - - la, dal -
life and love of - fend - ing De - ny to this right hand, Grant it to
mf
cresc.
p
cresc.
p
rit. molto.
la a'tuoi lu - mi, dal - - la, dal - la a'tuoi lu - mi.
thine, to thine own eyes, grant it to thine, to thine own eyes.
cresc.
p
rit. col canto.

Un certo non so che.

(There's one, I know him not.)

Arietta.

scen - do
f p
poco rit.
pur do - lor non è, do - lor non
yet no pain he brought, no pain he
scen do
sfz
p
poco rit.
Più sostenuto.
mf
è. Un cer - to non so che, un
brought. There's one, I know him not, there's
mf
animato. cresc.
cer - to non so che, non so che mi pas - sa il cor, e
one, I know him not, In - to my heart did rove, And
animato.
cresc.
f
cresc.
f p rit.
pur do - lor non è, e pur do - lor non
yet no pain he brought, and yet no pain he
cresc.
p rit.

p lento.
è.
brought.
Se que - sto fos - se a - mor?
Can this Un - known be Love?
f
p
col canto pp
f a tempo.
nel suo vo - ra - ce ar - dor,
Who, fain his pow'r to prove,
nel suo vo - ra - ce ar - dor già po - si in -
who, fain his pow'r to prove, A foot un -
f a tempo.
sfz
cau - ta, po - si il piè!
war - y, un - war - y caught!
Sostenuto espress.
a tempo.
se que - sto fos - se a - mor?
Can this Unknown be Love?
nel
Who,
cresc.
mf sostenuto.
a tempo.
suo vo - ra - ce ar - dor,
fain his pow'r to prove,
nel suo vo - ra - ce ar - dor già po - si in -
who, fain his pow'r to prove, A foot un -
mf
sfz

rfz
f
cau - ta, po - si il piè, in-cau - ta il piè!
war - y caught, a foot un-war - y caught!
cresc.
f
mf
ritard.
p molto ritard.
mf a tempo.
cresc.
Un cer-to non so che mi giun-ge e pas-sa il cor, mi
There's one, I know him not, In - to my heart did rove, in -
p
col canto.
p a tempo.
f
p
cresc.
giunge e passa il cor, e pur do - lor non è, e
to my heart did rove, And yet no pain he brought, and
p
cresc.
f
p
poco rit.
pur do - lor non è, do - lor non è.
yet no pain he brought, no pain he brought.
sfz
p
poco rit.

Più sostenuto.
mf
Un certo non so che, un certo non so
There's one, I know him not, there's one, I know him
mf
Ped. *
animato.
che, non so che mi pas-sa il cor, e
not, In-to my heart did rove, And
f
p
cresc. animato.
sfz
p
cresc.
portando.
pur do-lor non è, e
yet no pain he brought, and
cresc.
f
p
rit.
pur do-lor non è; mi giun-ge e pas-sa il
yet no pain he brought, in-to my heart did
rit.

cresc.
f
dim.
cor, mi giun-ge e pas-sa il cor, e pur do-
rove, in - to my heart did rove, And yet no
cresc.
f
mf
cresc. ed affettuoso.
lor non è, e pur do - lor non
pain he brought, and yet no pain he
dim.
p
più f
cresc.
ritard.
p
è, do - lor non è, do - lor non è!
brought, no pain he brought, no pain he brought!
col canto.
f
mf
dim.
p
f

Pur dicesti, o bocca bella.

(Mouth so charmful.)

Arietta.

English Version by
Dr TH. BAKER.

ANTONIO LOTTI.
(1667-1740)

11115

tr
dolce.
ca - ro sì, sì, che fa
lures me so, so, That in
ten.
ten.
tr rit.
tut - to il mio pia - cer, il mio pia - cer.
thee all bliss is mine, all bliss is mine.
rit.
a tempo
p
cresc.
Pur di - ce - sti, o
Mouth so charm-ful, O
a tempo
ben cantando.
cresc.
molto.
pp rit. con grazia.
boc - ca, boc - ca bel - la, o boc - ca, boc - ca bel - la,
tell me now, O tell me, O tell me now, O tell me
molto.
pp rit. col canto.

f
f
pp con grazia.
quel___ so - va - ve e ca - ro sì, sì, quel___ so -
Why___ thy sweet - ness lures___ me so, so, Why___ thy
ten.
portando cresc.
a - ve e ca - ro sì, che fa tut - to il mio pia -
sweet - ness lures me so, That in thee all___ bliss is
cresc.
mf
p smorz.
cer, il mi - o pia - cer,___ il mio pia -
mine, all bliss___ is___ mine,___ all bliss is___
dim.
p
tr
cer, quel___ so - a - ve e ca - ro sì, sì,
mine; Why___ thy sweet - ness lures___ me so, so,

smorz. con grazia.

f rit.

che — fa tut - to il mio pia - cer, — che — fa tut - to il
That — in thee all — bliss is mine, — that — in thee — all

rit.

cresc. *mf* smorz. dim.

mio — pia - cer, — il mio pia - cer.
bliss — is — mine, — all bliss is — mine.

p ben cantando.

mf

Per o -
E'en thy —

sempre *p*

nor di sua fa - cel - la con un — ba - cio A - mor t'a - prì, —
charms to vow com - pel me, Cu - pid — ope'd thee with a kiss, —

f

f

pp *rit.* *mf*

con — un — ba - cio A - mor — t'a - prì, — dol - ce —
Cu - pid — ope'd thee with — a — kiss, — Thou sweet

pp *rit.* *mf*

rit. *pp* *vocalizzato con grazia.*

fon - te — del go - der, ah! — ah!
fount of — joy di - vine, ah! — ah!

rit. col canto. *pp*

rit. *f* *rall.* *tr*

ah! — sì, — del go - der.
ah! — fount of joy di - vine.

rit. *f* *rall.*

p

Pur di -
Mouth so —

Tempo I.

p *ben cantando e legato.* *sempre p*

ce - sti, o boc - ca, boc - ca bel - la, o boc - ca, boc - ca
charm - ful, O tell me now, O tell me, O tell me now, O
tr
bel - la, quel so - a - ve e ca - ro sì,
tell me Why thy sweet - ness lures me so,
ten.
dolce.
sì, che fa tut - to il mio pia - cer, il
so, That in thee all bliss is mine, all
ten.
tr rit.
a tempo
mio pia - cer.
bliss is mine.
a tempo
rit.
ben cantando.

p
cresc. molto.
pp rit. con grazia.
Pur di - ce - sti, o boc - ca, boc - ca bel - la, o boc - ca, boc - ca
Mouth so charm - ful, O tell me now, O tell me, O tell me now, O
cresc. molto.
pp rit. col canto.
f
bel - la, quel so - a - ve e ca - ro sì, sì,
tell me Why thy sweet - ness lures me so, so,
ten.
pp con grazia.
rit.
portando.
cresc.
quel so - a - ve e ca - ro sì, che fa
Why thy sweet - ness lures me so, That in
pp
mf
tut - to il mio pia - cer, il mi - o pia - cer,
thee all bliss is mine, all bliss is mine,
dim.

p smorz.
tr
il mio pia - cer, quel so - a - ve e
all bliss is mine, Why thy sweet - ness
ten.
ca - ro sì, sì, che fa tut - to il mio pia-
lures me so, so, That in thee all bliss is
cresc.
smorz. con grazia.
rit.
cer, che fa tut - to il mio pia - cer, il
mine, that in thee all bliss is mine, all
mf smorz.
dim.
p
mio pia - cer.
bliss is mine.
ben cantando.

Sebben, crudele.

(Tho' not deserving.)

Canzonetta.

English Version by
Dr. TH. BAKER.

ANTONIO CALDARA.
(1671 - 1763)

11116

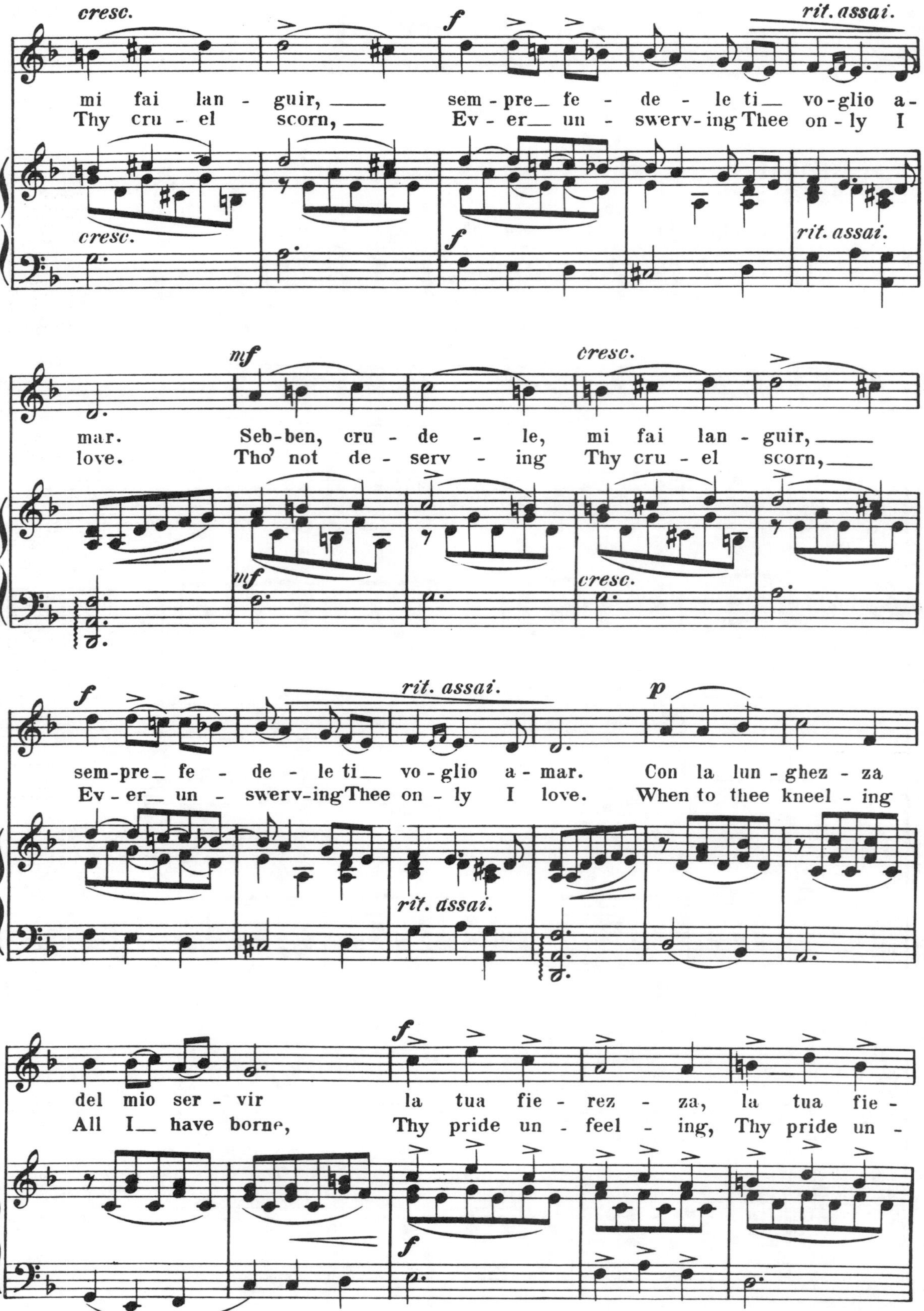
cresc.
f
rit. assai.
mi fai lan - guir, sem - pre_ fe - de - le ti_ vo - glio a -
Thy cru - el scorn, Ev - er_ un - swerv - ing Thee on - ly I
cresc.
f
rit. assai.
mf
cresc.
mar. Seb - ben, cru - de - le, mi fai lan - guir,
love. Tho' not de - serv - ing Thy cru - el scorn,
mf
cresc.
f
rit. assai.
p
sem - pre_ fe - de - le ti_ vo - glio a - mar. Con la lun - ghez - za
Ev - er_ un - swerv - ing Thee on - ly I love. When to thee kneel - ing
rit. assai.
f
del mio ser - vir la tua fie - rez - za, la tua fie -
All I_ have borne, Thy pride un - feel - ing, Thy pride un -
f

rez - za sa - prò stan - car, la tua fie - rez - za
feel - ing I — then shall move, Thy pride un - feel - ing
rit.
sa - prò stan - car.
I — then shall — move.
f
p smorz.
rit.
rit.
a tempo.
p
Seb - ben, cru - de - le, mi fai lan - guir, —
Tho' not de - serv - ing Thy cru - el scorn, —
p
cresc.
più cresc.
rit.
sem - pre fe - de - le, sem - pre fe - de - le ti vo - glio a -
Ev - er un - swerv - ing, ev - er un - swerving Thee on - ly I —
cresc.
più cresc..
rit.

mar.
love.
f deciso.
p
Seb - ben, cru -
Tho' not de -
mf
cresc.
f
de - le, mi fai lan - guir, sem - pre_ fe - de - le ti_
serv - ing Thy cru - el scorn, Ev - er_ un - swerv-ing Thee
rit assai.
mf
cresc.
vo - glio a - mar, seb - ben, cru - de - le, mi fai lan -
on - ly I love; Tho' not de - serv - ing thy cru - el
rit assai.
mf
cresc.
rit assai.
f
guir, sem - pre_ fe - de - le ti_ vo - glio a - mar.
scorn, Ev - er_ un - swerv-ing Thee on - ly I love.
f
rit assai.
pp
2 Ped.
*

Selve amiche, ombrose piante.
(Kindly forest.)

Arietta.

English Version by
Dr TH. BAKER.

ANTONIO CALDARA.
(1671 - 1763)

tratt. sempre e con grazia.
fi - do al - ber - go del mio co - re, del mio co - re, fi - do al - ber - go del mio
Ref-uge of mine heart con - fid - ing, of mine heart con-fid - ing, of mine heart con-
tratt. sempre e con grazia.
fi - do al - ber - - - - - - - go del mio
of mine heart, mine heart con-
co - - - - re,
fid - - - - ing:
p
chie - de a voi que -
Here a soul in
p
p
st'al - ma a - man - te qualche pa - ce, qualche pa - ce al suo do - lo -
love that parch - es, All her sor - row, all her sor - row would fain be hid -
cresc.
cresc.

cresc.
- - - re, qual-che pa - ce, qual - che pa - ce
- - - ing, All her sor - row, all her sor - row
cresc.
assai.
f rit.
p
al suo do-lo- - re. Sel - ve a - mi - che,
would fain be hid- - - ing. Kind - ly for - est,
assai.
f rit.
p
del mio co - re, del mio
heart, of mine heart con -
om - bro - se pian - te, fi - do al - ber - go del mio co- - -
ye shadowy arch - es, Ref - uge of mine heart con - fid- - -

co - - re, fi - do al - ber - go del mio co - re, del mio co - re, fi - do al -
fid - - ing, Ref - uge of mine heart con - fid - ing, of mine heart con - fid - ing,
- - - re, fi - do al - ber - - - - - - -
- - - ing, of mine heart,
ber - go del mio
of mine heart con -
- go del mio co - - - - - re.
mine heart con - fid - - - - ing.
rit.
tr
rit.
f a tempo.
rit. assai.

Come raggio di sol.
(As on the swelling wave.)

English Version by
Dr. TH. BAKER.

Aria.

ANTONIO CALDARA.
(1670 - 1763)

Sostenuto. (♩ = 46.)

Voice.

Piano.

cresc. molto.

ppp

dim.

pp

simili.

p

Co - me rag-gio di sol mi - te e se - re - no,
As on the swell-ing wave in i - dle mo - tion,

co - me rag-gio di sol mi - te e se - re - no
As on the swell-ing wave in i - dle mo - tion

so - vra pla- -ci - di flut - ti si ri - po- -sa,
Wan-ton sun - beams at play are gai - ly rid- -ing,

affrett. poco a poco.
pp
men - tre del ma - re, men - tre del ma - re nel pro -
While in the bosom, while in the bo - som of th'un-
affrett. poco a poco.
p
fon - do se - no sta la tem - pe -
fath - om'd o - cean There lies a tem -
p
cresc. e string.
f rit.
rall.
a tempo.
sta a sco - sa:
pest in hid - ing:
col canto.
p a tempo.
p
tranquillo.
co - sì ri - so ta - lor ga - io e pa - ca - to di con -
So are ma - ny that wear a mien con - tent - ed, Ma - ny a
pp

ten - to, di gio - ia un lab - bro in - fio - ra,
vis - age where - on a smile e'er hov - ers,
stent.
men - tre nel suo se - gre - to il cor pia - ga - - -
While, deep with - in, the bo - som a heart tor - ment - - -
cresc. e string.
stent.
f dim. e rit.
rall.
to s'an - go - scia e si mar - to - - -
ed In se - cret an - guish cov - -
f dim. e rit.
rall.
pp
ra.
ers.
dim. assai.
pp
ppp

Consolati e spera!

(Take heart again!)

English Version by
Dr. TH. BAKER.

Aria.

DOMENICO SCARLATTI.
(1685 - 1757)

spe - ra! po - trai d'al-tro og - get - to più lie - to go -
fal - ter! Thou'lt find one as charm-ing, Nor need she be
più f
dim. cresc. decresc.
der, go - der, più lie - -to go - der, più lie - to go - der! Con -
coy, be coy, nor need she be coy, nor need she be coy! Take
p cresc. mf dim.
ritard. ten. a tempo. cresc.
so - la - ti! po - trai d'al-tro og - get - -to più
heart a - gain! Thou'lt find one as charm - ing, Nor
col canto. f a tempo. cresc. f
ten. rfs rit. tr
lie- -to go - der, più lie - to go - - der.
need she be coy, nor need she be coy!
rit. col canto. rfz p pp f f

più f ben cantando e larga
La stel - la più
No star but may
marcato p smorz.
sf
legato.
mf
la frase.
fie - ra, se can - gia d'a - spet - to, può an-
al- -ter Its as - pect a - larm - ing, No
portando.
co - ra l'af - fan - no mu - ta - re in pia - cer, mu-
sor - row so last - ing but yield - eth to joy, but
cresc.
ta- - re in pia - cer, può an - co - ra l'af - fan - no, l'af - fan-
yield - eth to joy; No sor - row so last - ing, so last-
mf
f
sfz
p

a tempo.
a piacere.
rit.
no mu - ta - re in pia-cer! Con-so - la - ti! e
- ing but yield - eth to joy! Take heart a - gain! Ne'er
rit. a tempo. a piacere.
spe - ra! po - trai d'al-tro og - get - to più
fal - ter! Thou'lt find one as charm - ing, Nor
cresc.
poco marcato.
rit assai.
lie - to go - der, più lie - to go - der, con - so - la - ti!
need she be coy, nor need she be coy! Take heart a - gain!
rit. col canto.
più f
cresc.
e spe - ra! po - trai d'al-tro og - get - to più
ne'er fal - ter! Thou'lt find one as charm - ing, Nor
più f

lie - to go - der, go - der, più lie - to _ go - der, più lie - to go -
need she be coy, be _ coy, nor need _ she be coy, nor need _ she be
poco rit.
a tempo.
der! Con - so - la - ti! _ po - trai _ d'al - tro og - get - to più
coy! Take heart a - gain! _ Thou'lt find _ one as charm - ing, Nor
dim.
p col canto.
a tempo.
rfz
cresc.
ritard.
dolce e riten.
ten.
lie - to go - der, più lie - to, più lie - to go - der.
need she be coy, nor need she, nor need she be coy!
p col canto.
a tempo.
lento a piacere.
Spe - ra!
Take heart a - gain!
marcato.
smorz.
riten.

Affanni del pensier.

(O agonies of thought.)

Arietta.

English Version by
Dr TH. BAKER.

GIORGIO FEDERICO HANDEL.
(1683 _ 1751)

da - te - mi pa - ce almen,
leave me in peace a - gain,
da - te - mi pa - ce almen,
leave me in peace a - gain,
e
then
portando
poi tor - na - te.
turn and rend me.
Af - fan -
O ag -
f
- ni del pen - sier,
- o - nies of thought,
p smorz.
un sol mo - men - to
one mo - ment on - ly
mf
da - te - mi pa - ce almen,
leave me in peace a - gain,
e poi tor - na - te,
then turn and rend me,

un sol mo - men - to da - te - mi pa - ce al -
one mo - ment on - ly leave me in peace a -
men, e poi tor - na - te, tor - na - - - -
gain, then turn and rend me, one mo - - - -
te, e poi tor - na - te; Af - fan - ni del pen - sier,
ment, then turn and rend me; O ag - o - nies of thought,
da - te - mi pa - ce almen, e poi tor - na - te, e poi,
leave me in peace a - gain one moment on - ly, and then,

dim.
rit.
e po - i tor - na - - te.
then turn and rend me.
rit.
f
pp
rit. assai.

Ah! mio cor.

(Ah, poor heart.)

Aria.

English Version by
Dr TH. BAKER.

GIORGIO FEDERICO HANDEL.
(1683 - 1751)

Tempo I.
scher - ni - to se - i.
he scorns thy love.
Stel - le, De - i, Nu - me d'a - mo - re! tra - di -
Hear me, Heaven, ye gods a - bove! Thee, O
to - re, t'a - mo tan - to, puoi la - sciar - mi sola in
trai - tor, love I on - ly, Canst thou leave me weeping
pian - to? Oh De - i! puoi la - sciar - mi, oh
lone - ly? O Heaven! canst thou leave me, O

De - i, per - chè? t'a - mo tan - to,
Heav - en! and why? So I love thee,
puo - - i la - sciar - mi so - la, so - la,
canst thou leave me weeping, weeping,
f
p
l.h.
so - la in pian - to, puoi la - sciar - mi, oh De - i, per -
weeping and lone - ly, canst thou leave me, O Heav - en! and
chè?
why?
cresc.

f
Ah! mio co - re, scherni - to se - i. Stel - le,
Ah, poor heart! he scorns thy love. Hear me,
f
De - i, Nu - me d'a - mo - re! tra - di -
Heaven, ye gods a - bove! Thee, O
to - re, t'a - mo tan - to, puoi la - sciar - mi sola in
trai - tor, love I on - ly, Canst thou leave me weeping,
pian - to, oh De - - - i, puo - i la -
lone - ly, O Heav - - en! canst thou
sciar - mi so - la, so - la, so - la in pian - to,
leave me weeping, weeping, weeping, lone - ly,

puoi la - sciar - mi, oh De - i, per - chè? per-
canst thou leave me, O Heav - en, and why? and
chè? per - chè? puoi la - sciar - mi so - la in pian - to, oh
why? and why? canst thou leave me weeping, lone - ly, O
f largamente
rit.
De - i! puoi la - sciar - mi, oh De - i, per - chè?
Heav - en! canst thou leave me, O Heav - en, and why?
f largamente, col canto
f
riten. assai e ff

Il mio bel foco.

(My joyful ardor.)

Recitativo ed Aria.

English Version by
Dr. TH. BAKER.

BENEDETTO MARCELLO.
(1686 - 1739)

Allegretto affettuoso.
mf
Quella fiam-ma che m'ac-cen-de,
In my heart the flames that burn me,
mf
cresc.
p
mf
quel-la fiam-ma che m'ac-cen-de
in my heart the flames that burn me
più f
pia-ce tan-to all'al-ma mi-a,
All my soul do so en-rav-ish,
pia-ce tan-to all'al-ma mi-a,
all my soul do so en-ravish,
sf
sf
rit.
f portando
che giammai s'e-stin-gue-rà, s'e-stin-gue-rà, s'e-stin-gue-
That they ne'er shall cease to glow, shall cease to glow, shall cease to
sf
p
rit.

p dolcemente legato e cresc.
sf
rà, pia-ce tanto al - l'al - ma - mi - a che giam - mai s'e - stin - gue -
glow, All my soul do so en - rav-ish, That they ne'er shall cease to
p
cresc. sempre
rà, s'e - stin - gue - rà, che giam - mai s'e - stin - gue -
glow, shall cease to glow, that they ne'er shall cease to
p
cresc. sempre
f
p rit.
a tempo
rà, s'e - stin - gue - rà, s'e - stin - gue - rà.
glow, shall cease to glow, shall cease to glow.
f
p col canto
a tempo
cresc.
p legato con grazia
E se il fato a voi mi
And should fate to ye re -
f
p dim. smorz.
p

ren-de, va - ghi rai del mio bel so - le, al - tra luce el - la non
turn me, Wan - d'ring rays of my fair sun, Oth - er light I cov - et
vuo - le nè vo - ler giammai po - trà, nè vo -
none, Nor the wish can ev - er know, nor the
(or.)
cresc. poco a poco
ler giammai po - trà, nè vo - ler, nè vo - ler giam -
wish can ev - er know, nor the wish, nor the wish can
cresc. poco a poco
mai po - trà, giammai po - trà, nè vo - ler giammai po -
ev - er know, can ev - er know, nor the wish can ev - er
rit.
col canto

trà.
know.
a tempo
cresc.
p
Quel-la fiam-ma che m'ac-cen-de pia-ce tanto al-l'al-ma
In my heart the flames that burn me All my soul do so en-
p
mi-a, pia-ce tanto al-l'al-ma mi-a, che giammai s'e-stin-gue-
ravish, all my soul do so en-ravish That they ne'er shall cease to
rit.
mf
rà, s'e-stin-gue-rà, s'e-stin-gue-rà, pia-ce tanto al-l'al-ma
glow, shall cease to glow, shall cease to glow; All my soul do so en-
f rit.

cresc.
mi-a che_ giam-mai s'e-stin-gue-rà,_ s'e-stin - gue-rà, che giam-
ravish, That they ne'er shall cease to glow, shall cease to glow, that they
f rit.
a tempo
mai s'e - stin - gue-rà, s'e-stin-gue-rà,_ s'e - stin-gue-
ne'er shall cease to_ glow, shall cease to glow, shall_ cease to_
col canto
a tempo
p dolce
rà, quel-la_ fiam-ma_ giammai, giammai s'e - stin - gue-
glow, that they_ ne'er shall_ cease, that they ne'er shall cease_ to
f
rinforz. e rit.
a tempo
rà.
glow.
mf
a tempo
f rit.

Ogni pena più spietata.

(All of anguish most unsparing.)

English Version by
Dr. TH. BAKER.

Arietta.

GIOVANNI B. PERGOLESI.
(1710 - 1736)

sof - fri - ria que - st'al - ma af - flit - ta e de - so - la - ta,
Fain would bear this soul for - sak - en And de - spair - ing,
tratt. cresc. ed animando
f
mf
se go - desse u - na spe - ran - za di po - ter - si con - so - lar. ah,
if her hope remain'd un - shak - en To con - sole herself once more. ah,
col canto
cresc.
p
p con grazia.
rit.
ah, di po - ter - si con - so - lar, di po - ter - si con - so - lar.
ah, to con - sole herself once more, to con - sole her - self once more.
col canto.
mf
p
O - gni
All of
tr
p

pe - na più spie - ta - ta, più spie - ta - ta sof - fri -
an - guish most un - spar - ing, most un - spar-ing Fain would
ri - a que - st'al - ma af - flit - ta e de - so - là - ta, o - gni
bear this soul for - sak - en And de - spair-ing; all of
rit.
tratt.
pe - na più spie - ta - ta sof - fri - ria quest'alma af - flit - ta, se go -
anguish most un - sparing Fain would bear this soul for - sak - en, If her
rit.
col canto.
cresc. ed animando assai
desse u - na spe - ran - za di po - ter - si con - so - lar. ah,
hope remain'd un - shak - en To con - sole her-self once more. ah,
cresc.

p
p con grazia.
poco rit.
ah,_ di po-ter-si_con-so-lar, di po-ter-si con-so-lar.
ah,_ to con-sole herself once more, to con-sole herself once more.
Poco più mosso.
col canto.
mf
p
f
p
Tempo I.
p
Ma, ohi-mè, ca-de o-gni speme, non c'è luo-go, non c'è vi-ta, non c'è
But, a-las, how endless my torment, There's no vi-sion, there's no moment, There's no
p
f ritenuto un poco.
p
mo-do di spe-rar, non c'è mo-do_ di spe-rar, non c'è mo-do di spe-
ray_ of hope in store, there's no ray of hope in store, there's no ray of hope in
col canto.

rar.
store.
Tempo I.
O - gni pe - na più spie - ta - ta, più spie -
All of an - guish most un - spar - ing, most un -
ta - ta sof - fri - ri - a que - st'al - ma af - flit - ta e
spar - ing Fain would bear this soul for - sak - en
de - so - la - ta, o - gni pe - na più spie - ta - ta sof - fri -
And de - spair-ing, all of an - guish most un - spar-ing, Fain would

rit.
poco rit.
cresc. ed animando.
ria_ que-st'alma af - flit - ta, se go - des-se u - na spe - ran - za di po -
bear this soul for - sak - en If her hope remain'd un - shak - en To con -
col canto.
col canto.
cresc.
f
mf
p
ter - si con - so - lar,_ ah,_ ah,_ di po - ter - si con - so -
sole her-self once more; ah,_ ah,_ to con - sole her-self once
ritenuto assai.
lar, di po - ter - si_con - so - lar.
more, to con - sole her-self once more.
Poco più mosso.
col canto.
f
p
f
f
rit.
tr

Stizzoso, mio stizzoso.

(Unruly, Sir, unruly?)

English Version by
Dr. TH. BAKER.

Aria.

GIOVANNI B. PERGOLESI.
(1710 - 1736)

che - - to, che - - to; e non par - la - re,
qui - - et, qui - - et, And now keep si-lence,
zit_ zit_ Ser - pi - na_ vuol co - sì, zit_
hush! hush! Ser - pi - na_ you'll o - bey; hush!
zit_ Ser - pi - na_ vuol co - sì.
hush! Ser - pi - na_ you'll o - bey!
Stiz - zo - so, mio_ stiz -
Un - ru - ly, Sir,_ un -

zo-so, voi fa-te il bo-ri-o-so, ma no,
ru-ly, And fain to play the bul-ly? But naught,
ma non vi può gio-va-re; bi-so-gna al mio di-vie-to star
naught you'll gain by vio-lence; 'Tis time to end this ri-ot, Be
che-to, che-to; e non par-la-re,
qui-et, qui-et, And now keep si-lence;
zit zit Ser-pi-na vuol co-sì, voi
hush! hush! Ser-pi-na you'll o-bey. You

fa-te il bo-ri - o - so, ma non vi può gio - va - re, bi - sogna al mio di -
fain would play the bul-ly, But naught you'll gain by violence; 'Tis time to end this
vie - to star che-to e non par - la - re, zit zit
ri - ot; Be qui - et, and keep si - lence, hush! hush!
che - to, zit zit e non par - lar, Ser -
qui - et! hush! hush! keep si - lence now, Ser -
pi - na vuol co - sì, vuol co - sì, Ser - pi - na
pi - na you'll o - bey, you'll o - bey, Ser - pi - na
f
pp

vuol co - sì.
you'll o - bey!
Cre -
I
d'io che m'in-ten - de-te, sì, che m'inten - de-te, sì, che m'inten-
think you com-pre - hend me,yes! you compre-hend me,yes! you compre-
de-te, da che mi co-no - sce-te son mol-ti e mol-ti dì, son
hend me, For you've not dared of - fend me This ma-ny and many a day, this
mol - ti, mol - ti e mol - ti dì.
ma - ny, ma - ny, this ma - ny a day.

Stiz - zo - so, mio stiz - zo - so, voi fa - te il bo - ri - o - so, ma no, ma non vi può gio - va - re; ma no, ma non vi può gio -
Un - ru - ly, Sir, un - ru - ly, And fain to play the bul - ly? But naught, naught you'll gain by vio-lence, But naught, naught you'll gain by
p
f
tr

p
va - re; bi - so-gna al mio di - vie-to star che - - to,
vio-lence;'Tis time to end this ri - ot; Be qui - - et,
p
p
pp
che - - to; e non par - la - re, zit_ zit_
qui - - et; And now keep si-lence, hush! hush!
pp
f
pp
f
Ser-pi - na_ vuol co - sì, zit_ zit_ Ser-pi - na_
Ser-pi - na_you'll o - bey! hush! hush! Ser-pi - na_
f
pp
f
vuol co - sì. Stiz-
you'll o - bey! Un-

zo - so, mio_stiz - zo-so, voi fa-te il bo-ri - o-so, ma
ru - ly, Sir,_un - ru-ly, And fain to play the_ bul-ly? But
p
no, ma non vi può gio-va-re: bi - so-gna al mio di - vie-to star
naught, naught you'll gain by vio-lence;'Tis time to end this ri-ot; Be
f
p
che - - to, che - - to; e non par - la-re, zit_
qui - - et, qui - - et; And now keep si-lence; hush!
pp
p
pp
zit_ Ser-pi-na_vuol co - sì, voi fa-te il bo-ri - o-so, ma
hush! Ser-pi-na_you'll o - bey! You fain would play the bul-ly, But
f
f

non vi può gio - va - re, bi - sogna al mio di - vie-to star che-to e non par-
naught you'll gain by vio-lence; 'Tis time to end this ri - ot; Be qui-et, and keep
la - re, zit_ zit_ che - to, zit_ zit_
si - lence; hush! hush! qui - et! hush! hush!
e non par - lar. Ser - pi - na vuol co - sì, vuol co-
keep si - lence now. Ser - pi - na wills it so, wills it
sì, Ser-pi - na_vuol co - sì.
so, Ser-pi - na_wills it so!
f
pp
ff
tr

Se tu m'ami, se sospiri
(If thou lov'st me.)

Arietta.

English Version by
Dr. TH. BAKER.

GIOVANNI B. PERGOLESI.
(1710 - 1736)

a tempo
che_so-let-to Io_ti-deb-ba ri - a-mar, Pa-sto-rel - lo, sei sog-get-to
that demure-ly I_on thee a - lone_may smile, Simple shepherd,thou art sure-ly
a tempo
pp
cresc.
Fa - cil-mente_a t'in-gannar; Pa-sto-rel-lo, sei sog-get-to Fa - cil - men-te_a
Prone thy sens-es to beguile; Simple shepherd,thou art surely Prone thy senses_
p
cresc.
p
t'in-gan-nar, Fa - cil - men - te_a_ t'in-gan-nar. Bel-la ro-sa
to be-guile, prone thy_ sens - es_ to be-guile. As a fair red
p
poco cresc.
por-po - ri - na Og - gi Sil-via sce - glie - rà, Con la scu - sa
rose, a_ lov- er Fain might Sil-via choose to - day, Hap-ly if_ he

sempre cresc.
del - la spi - na Do - man poi la sprez - ze - rà, Doman poi la__ sprez - ze - rà.
thorns dis - cov - er 'Tis to - morrow thrown a - way, 'Tis to - mor - row thrown a - way.
sempre cresc.
cresc. un poco
Ma de - gli uomi - ni il __ con - si - glio Io per me non se - gui - rò. Non perchè mi
All men say of maid - en - fol - ly Finds no fa - vor in mine eyes, Nor because I
cresc. un poco
rit.
pia - ce il gi - glio Gli al - tri fio - ri sprez - ze - rò.
love the lil - y Shall I oth - er flow'rs de - spise.
a tempo
rit.
p
p
cresc.
Se tu__ m'a - mi, se tu so - spi - ri Sol per
If thou lov'st me, and sigh - est ev - er But for
p
cresc.

rit.
p a tempo
me, gen-til pa - stor, Ho do-lor de' tuoi mar-ti-ri, Ho di-let-to
me, O gen-tle swain, Sweet I find thy lov-ing fa-vor, Pi-ti-ful I
f rit.
del tuo a-mor, Ma se-pen-si che so-let-to Io ti-deb-ba ri - a-mar,
feel thy pain. Should'st thou think tho', that de-mure-ly I on thee a-lone may smile,
a tempo
pp
Pa-sto-rel-lo, sei sog-get-to Fa-cil-mente a t'in-gannar, Pa-sto-rel-lo,
Simple shepherd, thou art sure-ly Prone thy sens-es to beguile; Simple shepherd,
p
cresc.
rit. assai
sei sog-get-to Fa-cil-mente a t'in-gannar, Fa-cil-mente a t'in-gannar.
thou art sure-ly Prone thy sens-es to beguile, prone thy sens-es to beguile.

O del mio dolce ardor.

(O thou belov'd.)

Aria.

English Version by
Dr. TH. BAKER.

CRISTOFORO GLUCK.
(1714 - 1787)

p
L'au - ra che tu re - spi - - ri,
At length the air thou breath - - est
al - fin re - spi - - ro,
my soul in - spir - - eth,
f
al - - fin re -
my soul in -
f

spi - - - - - - ro. O -
spir - - - - - - eth. Wher -
vun - que il guar - do io gi - - - ro, Le tue
e'er mine eye may wan - - - der, Still of
va - ghe sem - bian - ze A - mo - re in me di - pin - ge: Il
thee some vague sem - blance Doth Love a-wake with-in me, My
mio pen - sier si fin - ge Le più lie - - -
ev - 'ry thought doth win me To yet fond - - -
cresc.

f
dim. assai.
te spe- ran - ze;
er re - mem - brance;
f
dim.
p
E nel de - si - o che co - sì
And in this ar - dor that all my
p
m'em - pie il pet - to
bo - som so fir - eth
p
Cer - co te,
Thee I seek,
cresc.
chia - mo te,
Thee I call,
dolce.
p ten. pp
spe - ro e so -
Fond - ly and e'er
pp
p col canto pp

(a piacere)
spi - - - - - ro. Ah! O del mio dol - ce ar -
fond - - - - - er. Ah! O thou be - lov'd whom
dor bra - ma - to og - get - - to, bra - ma - to og -
long my heart de - sir - - eth, my heart de -
get - - - - to, L'au - ra che tu re -
sir - - - eth, At length the air thou

spi - - ri, al - fin re -
breath - - est my soul in -
spi - - - - ro, al -
spir - - - - eth, my
fin, al - fin re - spi - - - - - ro.
soul, my soul in - spir - - - - - eth.

Chi vuol comprar la bella calandrina.

(Who will buy the beautiful canary.)

English Version by
H. MILLARD.

NICCOLO JOMMELLI.
(1714-1774)

f
can - ta da mat - ti - no in fi - no a se - ra? Chi — vuol, chi — vuol com -
sings from ear - ly morn to eve so gai - ly? Who wish - es — now to
prar - la, ven - ga a con - trat - to! Ven - ga!
buy — her? Come, make an of - fer! Come — now!
ven - ga! Sempre a buon pat - to — la — ven - de -
come — now! A bar - gain 'tis, such as — ne'er — was
rò, Sempre a buon pat - to — la — ven - de - - rò. La
seen, a bar - gain 'tis, such as — ne'er — was seen. The
p
tr

bel-la ca-lan-dri - - na! chi vuol, chi vuol com - prarla?
beauti-ful ca - na - - ry! Who wish-es now to buy her?
chi? chi? Ven - ga! ven ga! Sem - pre a buon
Who? who? Come now! come now! A bar - gain
pat - to la ven - de - rò, Sem - pre a buon pat - to la ven - de -
'tis, such as ne'er was seen, a bar - gain 'tis, such as ne'er was
ro. E
seen. So

sì gentil, ha_ co - sì dol - ce il can - - to, E ven - der - la deg -
pretty, too, and sings so sweet and clear - - ly, Al - tho' I sell her,
g'io che l'a - mo tan - to; Ma que - sto è il mio me - stie - re, No'l fo per pia -
still I love her dear - ly; But 'tis to _ earn a liv - ing, Not for pleasure
ce - re! Ven - ga! ven - ga! Sempre a buon pat - to _ la _
striving! Come now, come now! A bargain 'tis, such as _
ven - de - rò, Sempre a buon pat - to _ la _ ven - de - rò. La
ne'er _ was seen, a bar - gain 'tis, such as _ ne'er _ was seen. The
tr
f
p

bel-la ca-lan-dri - - na! chi vuol, chi vuol com - prarla?
beauti-ful ca- na - - ry! Who wish-es now to — buy her?
chi? chi? Ven-ga! ven-ga! Semprea buon
Who? who? Come now! come now! A bar-gain
pat - to - la - ven - de - rò, Semprea buon pat - to - la - ven - de -
'tis, such as - ne'er - was seen, a bar-gain 'tis, such as - ne'er - was
rò.
seen.

Ombra cara, amorosa.
(Gentle Shade, well beloved.)
Scena ed Aria.

English Version by
Dr. TH. BAKER.

TOMMASO TRAETTA.
(1727 – 1779)

mf sost.
Tu tran-
All the
sost.
quil-la godra - i nel-le se-di be - a - te, o - ve non
calm now enjoy - est thou Of th'a-bode of the bless - ed, where-to ex-
f
decresc.
giun-ge nè sde-gno, nè do - lor; nè sde-gno, nè do - lor; do - ve ri-
tendeth Nor sor-row nor dis - tress, nor sor-row nor dis-tress; wherefrom are
p
p legatissimo.
co - pre o-gni cu-ra mor-ta - le e-ter-no ob-blì -
ban - ish'd All the cares of this earth, and ef-fac'd for ev -
rit.
rit.

mf
o, nè più rammen-te-ra - i,
er, Un-heedful wherethounev - er
cresc.
cresc.
fra gli am-ples - si pa-ter - ni il pian-to mi - o, nè
In thy fa-ther's em-brac - es shalt hear my la-ment - ing, Re-
cresc.
que - sto di do-lor, nè que - sto di do-lor sog -
call no sor - row, re - call no sor - row where -
cresc.
f
pp tranquillo.
tr
gior - no in-fe - sto. Om-bra ca-ra a-mo-ro - sa, ah! per-chè ma-i tu
of thou hast partak - en. Gen-tle Shade well be-lov - ed, ah, wherefore hast thou To
f
pp

f
mf
rit.
cor-ri al tuo ri-po-so, ed io qui re- sto?
thy re-pose de-part-ed, and me for- sak- en?
Andantino. (♪ = 108.)
p grazia.
Io re-sto sem-pre a pian-ge-re do-ve mi gui-da o-
I still un-hap-py am wan-der-ing Whith-er my fate may
p
mf p
gnor, do-ve mi gui-da o-gnor
e'er, Whith-er my fate may e'er
f
d'un in un al- tro or- ror,
Deep-er in dark de- spair.
fp

f
d'un in un al - tro or - ror
deeper in dark de - spair
f
la cru-da sor -
Cru-el-ly lead
te.
me.
mf
E a ter - mi - nar le
And ne'er shall cease my
f
f
la - grime, pie - to - sa al mi - o do - lor, ahi! che non giunge an -
pi - ti - ful, My mourn-ful tears to flow, Nor aught of joy I
p
mf
p
f
rit. p
mf
cresc.
cor - per me la mor - te, io re - sto sem-pre a
know, Till death has freed me. I still un-hap-py am
f
col canto.
p animato.
cresc.

pian-ge-re, e a ter-mi-nar le la-grime, pie-to-sa al mi-o do-
wan-der-ing, And ne'er shall cease my pi-ti-ful, My mournful tears to
lor, ahi! che non giunge an-cor per me la mor-
flow, Nor aught of joy I know, Till death has freed
rit. col canto.
te, non giun-ge an-cor per me la mor-te, per me la mor-
me; Nor aught of joy I know Till death, till death has freed
rit.
te, per me la mor- te.
me, till death has freed me.
rit. assai.

O notte, o Dea del mistero.

(O night, mysterious Goddess.)

Aria.

English Version by
Dr TH. BAKER.

NICCOLÒ PICCINNI.
(1728 - 1800)

dou - ce com - pa - gne de l'a - mour, O
dol - ce com - pa - gna d'a - mor, O
Love's dear com - pan - ion and friend, O
nuit, c'est en toi que j'es - pè - re!
not - - te, è in te so - la ch'io spe - ro!
night, I can hope in thee on - ly!
hâ - te - toi de chas - ser le
deh scac - - cia del gior - no il ful -
Haste, O hast - - en, that day do
jour; hâ - te - toi
gor; deh scac - - - -
end; Haste, O hast - - -
mf
pp
cresc.
p
più f
sf

de chas - ser le jour, de chas - ser le jour, de chas - ser le
cia del gior-no il ful - gor, del gior-no il ful - gor, del gior-no il ful -
en, that day do end, that day do end, that day do
Un poco animato con affetto.
jour.
gor.
end.
Char - mant es
O spe -
O bliss - ful
Un poco animato.
poir, cru - el mar -
me, cru - del mar -
hope, O cru - el an -
ty - re,
ti - ro,
guish,
cresc.
mo - ment de
oi - stan -
O hours of

trou - - - - - - -ble et de bon -
te di gau-dio e ti -
joy and of de -
decresc.
heur, et de bon- -heur, je
mor, di gau - dio e ti- -mor, io
spair, and of de - -spair, I
più f
crains, je trem- -ble, je dé -
te- -mo, io tre- -mo, e de -
fear, I trem- -ble, I
cresc.
si- -re, je trem- -ble, je dé -
si- -ro, io tre - -mo, e de -
lan- -guish, I trem- -ble, I

sf
p
si- - - -re et mon coeur tour à tour sou-
si- - - -ro e d'a-mo-re so-spi-ra, so-
lan- - - -guish, And my heart sighs in love, sighs in
f
p
cresc.
pi-re d'a-mour, d'es-poir et de fra-yeur, d'es-
spi-ra il mio cor, di spe-me e di ti-mor, di
love it doth share With hope and with de-spair, with
cresc.
f
poir et de fra-yeur, et de fra-
spe- - me e di ti-mor, e di ti-
hope and with de-spair, and with de-
sf
più tranquillo.
f
p
yeur. O nuit, Dé-
mor. O not-te, o
spair. O night, mys-
f
p
p

es - se du mys - tè - re, dou - ce com - pa-gne de l'a-
de - a del mi - ste - ro, dol - ce com - pa - gna d'a-
te-rious God - dess lone - ly, Love's dear com - pan - ion and
mf
espress.
sf
più f
mour, O nuit, o
mor, O not- -te, o
friend, O night, O
p
p
nuit, c'est en toi que j'es - pè - re,
not- -te, è in te so- -la ch'io spe - ro,
night, I can hope in thee on - ly,
più f
più f
sf
hâ - te - toi de chas - ser le jour, O
deh scac - cia del gior-no il ful - gor, ah!
Haste, O hast - en, that day do end, O
sf
f

nuit, c'est en toi, en toi que j'es - pè - re, hâ - te-
sì, del gior- -no il ful - gor, del
night, I can hope, I can hope in thee on - ly, Haste, O
mf
p
con affetto.
allargando.
rit.
ten.
toi de chasser le jour, de chas - ser le jour, de chasser le
gior- -no il ful - gor, del gior-no il ful - gor, del gior-no il ful -
hast-en, that day do end, that day do end, that day do
f
allargando.
col canto.
jour.
gor.
end.
a tempo.
più f

Chi vuol la zingarella.

(Who'll try the Gipsy pretty.)

Canzone.

English Version by
Dr. TH. BAKER.

GIOVANNI PAISIELLO.
(1741 - 1816)

so bene in-do-vi-nar. I giovani al can-to - ne
Their fortune I can tell; The laddies at the inn, too,
so meglio stuzzi - car. A vecchi in-na-mo-ra-ti scal - dar fo le cer -
I can amuse as well. When old men feel love burning, I set their heads a -
vel - la, scal - dar fo le cer - vel - la, a vecchi inna - mo - ra - ti. Chi
turning, I set their heads a - turn-ing, When old men feel love burn - ing. Who'll
rit.
tr
p
sf
vuol la zin-ga - rel-la, chi vuol la zin-ga - rel-la? Si - gnori, ec - co - la
try the Gip-sy pretty, Who'll try the Gip-sy pretty? Come one and all to

p
qua, si - gnori, ec - co - la — qua. Le don-ne sul bal -
me, come one and all — to — me. For ladies at their
p
pp
co - ne so bene in-do-vi - nar. I giovani al can-
win - dow Their fortune I can tell, The laddies at the
to - ne so meglio stuzzi - car. A vecchi in-na - mo -
inn, too, I can amuse as well. When old men feel love
f p
rit.
ra - ti, a vecchi in-na-mo - ra - ti scal - dar fo — le cer-vel-la. Chi
burn - ing I set their heads a - turn - ing, I — set their heads a - turning. Who'll
col canto
f p f p

a tempo
vuol la zin - ga - rel - la gra - zio - sa, ac - cor - ta e
try the Gip - sy pret - ty, So win - ning, wise and
a tempo
bel - la? Si - gno - ri, ec - co - la qua; si -
wit - ty, As one and all may see, as
gno - ri, ec - co - la qua, gra - zi - o - sa, ac - cor - ta e
one and all may see; So win - ning, wise and
bel - la, gra - zi - o - sa, accor - ta e bel - la. Si - gno - ri, ec - co - la
wit - ty, so winning, wise and wit - ty, As one and all may
f
p

qua, gra - zi - o - sa, ac - cor - ta e
see, so winning and so
bel - la, gra - zi - o - sa, ac - cor - ta e
wit - ty, so winning, wise and
f
p
animando sempre e cresc.
bel - la, Si - gno - ri, ec - co - la
wit - ty, As one and all may
qua, si - gno - ri, si -
see, so winning, so
f
p
animando sempre e cresc.
gno - ri, si - gno - ri, ec - co - la
wit - ty, As one and all may
qua, si - gno - ri, si -
see? so win - ning, so
rit.
gnori, si - gnori, ec - co - la qua.
wit - ty, Come one and all to me.
rit.
f

Nel cor più non mi sento.

(Why feels my heart so dormant.)

Arietta.

mor, sei col - pa tu. Mi piz - zi-chi, mi stuz-zi-chi, mi
Love, the fault_ is thine! He teas - es me, he pinches me, He
pun - gi-chi, mi mas - ti - chi; che co - sa è que - sto ahi - mè? pie -
squeezes me, he wrenches me; What tortures I must bear! Have
sf
tà, pie - tà, pie - tà! a - mo - re è un cer - to che, che
done, have done, have done! Thou, Love, art sure - ly one Will
p
risoluto
di - spe - rar - mi fa.
drive me to de - spair!
f

Il mio ben quando verrà.
(When, my love, wilt thou return.)

English Version by
Dr. TH. BAKER.

Aria.

GIOVANNI PAISIELLO.
(1741-1816)

Andante. (♩= 44.)

Piano.

Voice.

p dolce

Il mi - o ben quan - do ver - rà
When, my love, wilt thou re - turn,

a ve - der la me - sta a - mi - ca?
Her to see for thee who is sigh - ing?

di bei fior s'am - man - - te - rà la
On the shore the sun doth burn, The
spiag - gia, la spiag-gia a - - pri - - - ca.
flow - ers, the flow-ers are dy - - - ing,
Ma nol ve - do,
But my lov - er,
ma nol ve - do,
but my lov - er
e il mio ben, ahi - mè! non
ne'er I see re - turn, Woe's

vien? e' il mio ben, ahi-mè! non
me! Ne'er I see re-turn! Woe's
vien? e il mio ben ahi-mè! non vien?
me! ne'er I see re-turn! Woe's me!
Men - tre al - l'au - re spie - ghe - rà
While his sweet-heart on the air
la sua fiamma, i suo - i la - men - ti,
Wastes her sor-row in pi - ti - ful cry - ing,
mi - ti au - ge - i v'in - se - gne - rà più
Re - spon - sive moun-tains her plaint will bear, More

dol - ci, più dol - ci ac - cen - ti.
gen - tly, more gen - tly re - ply - ing.
Ma non l'o - do.
Who can hear him?
E chi l'u - dì?
No voice hear I!
Ah! il mio be - ne am - mu - to - lì.
Ah! still my lov - er makes no re - ply.
Ah! am - mu - to - lì.
Ah! makes no re - ply.
3

Tu cui stan - ca o - ma - i già fe'
Kind - ly ech - o, whose pa - tience with me
il mio pian - to, e - co pie - to - sa,
My com - plain - ings al - read - y do tire,
ei ri - tor - na e dol - ce a te
Now re - turn them, and gen - tly to thee
chie - de, chie - de la spo -
Draw thou my fond de - sire.

sa.
Pian, mi chia - ma;
Hark! he calls me;
pp
sempre ppp
pia - no ahi - mè! pia - no, ahi-
hark! woe's me! hark! woe's
cresc.
mè! no, non mi chia-ma, oh Di-o, oh
me! No, he does not call me, O heav-en, O
f
p
f p
Di-o, non c'è.
heav-en, 'tis not he!

Plaisir d'amour.

(The Joys of Love.)

English Version by
H. MILLARD.

GIOVANNI MARTINI.
(1741 - 1816)

mour du - re tou - te la vi - - e.
mor tut - ta la vi - ta du - - ra.
bit - ter thro' a life - - time prove.
p
mf
J'ai tout quit -
Tut - to scor - dai per
I gave up
mf
té pour l'in - gra - te Syl - vi - - e;
le - i, per Sil - via in - fi - - da;
all for cru - el Syl - via's love,
cresc.
f
dim.
p
el - - le me quit - te et prend un au - tre a -
el - - la or mi scor - da e ad al - tro a - mor s'af - fi -
Too soon I find an - oth - er owns her
cresc.
dim.

mant.
da.
heart.
Plai-sir d'a-
Pia-cer d'a-
The joys of
mf
dim.
p rit.
mour ne du - re qu'un mo - ment: cha-
mor più che un dì sol non du - ra: mar-
love e'er swift - ly do de - part, Its
grin d'a - mour du-re tou-te la vi -
tir d'a - mor tut-ta la vi-ta du -
sor - rows bit - ter thro' a life time
rit.
e.
ra.
prove.
rit. assai.
p
p

mf
"Tant que cet-te eau - cou - le - ra dou - ce - ment vers
"Fin - chè tran-quil - lo scor - re - rà il ru - scel là
"Long as this brook - let shall soft - ly on - ward flow, The
dolce.
cresc.
f
ce ruisseau qui bor - de la prai - ri - e je t'ai - me-
ver-so il mar che cin - ge la pia - nu - ra io t'a - me-
mead - ow pass - ing on its joy - ous way, Thee I will
cresc.
f
f
mf
mf
rai," me ré - pé - tait Syl - vi - e.
rò," mi dis - se l'in - fe - de - le.
love," ev - er would Syl - via say:
pp e smorz.
rinf. e rit.
L'eau cou - le en - cor, el - le a chan - gé pour-
Scor - re il ri - o an - cor, ma can - giò in lei l'a-
Still flows the stream, but chang'd is Syl - via
pp

con dolore
tant.
mor.
now.
Plai - sir d'a -
Pia - cer d'a -
The joys of
mour ne du - re qu'un mo - ment: cha - grin d'a -
mor più che un dì sol non du - ra: mar - tir d'a -
love e'er swift - ly do de - part, Its sor - rows
più f
cresc. rall. rit.
mour du - re tou - te la vi - - e.
mor tut - ta la vi - ta du - - ra.
bit - ter, bit - ter thro' a life - time prove.
sf
mf
p
rit.
cresc.